PRAC[...] HANDB[...] FAIR LENDING FOR BANK DIRECTORS AND EXECUTIVE OFFICERS

SECOND EDITION

AMERICAN ASSOCIATION OF BANK DIRECTORS

DAVID BARIS,
LORI SOMMERFIELD,
CHRIS WILLIS & SARAH PRUETT

These materials and commentary are intended for educational purposes only. No portion may be construed as rendering legal advice for specific cases, or as creating an attorney-client relationship between the audience and the authors. The opinions expressed herein are solely those of the authors.

American Association of Bank Directors
National Capital Office
14400 Falling Leaf Drive
Darnestown, MD 20878

www.AABD.org

Preface

This book, now in its Second Edition, updates how bank boards of directors can provide meaningful oversight of fair lending risk management. It also describes best practices to enhance banks' fair lending compliance programs and to meet regulatory expectations.

Fair lending risks are ever present and increasing. The role of bank boards of directors to oversee these risks is essential. Their role in supporting robust fair lending risk management efforts and "setting the tone" at the top of the organization can make a real difference.

It's more than just controlling fair lending risk; it's also being fair in all respects to customers and prospective customers. As a bank director recently told me, "It's just the right thing to do."

The book is not only a primer for bank directors; it also is a resource for many others, including CEOs, chief risk officers, chief compliance officers, and fair lending officers and their staffs.

Outside directors have livelihoods outside of serving as a board member. They often have limited time to spend on any particular topic. Those directors who do not wish to read the book in its entirety may decide to read at least Chapters I and II.

The board of directors could also designate one member of the board who is also a member of the risk or compliance committee to read the entire book and become a resource on fair lending for the entire board.

For the chief compliance officer or fair lending officer, there is no escape hatch – read the book in its entirety and refer to it often as a resource!

I wish to thank my co-authors – Lori Sommerfield, Chris Willis, and Sarah Pruett at the law firm of Troutman Pepper Hamilton Sanders LLP ("Troutman Pepper") – for their time and effort in updating and rewriting the book. Many thanks also to Christine Emello and Teri Townsend at Troutman Pepper for proofreading and cite-checking of the book, respectively.

The biographies of the co-authors can be found at the end of the book as well as information on Troutman Pepper's outstanding consumer financial services practice.

David Baris, President
American Association of Bank Directors

TABLE OF CONTENTS

CHAPTER I.   AN INTRODUCTION TO FAIR LENDING

Although the concept of fair lending has existed since the late 1960s, over the past decade the industry has witnessed a dramatic shift in the regulatory landscape for enforcement of the federal fair lending laws. Non-compliance with fair lending laws — as well as allegations that a bank's lending practices are discriminatory — can damage a bank's reputation, lead to regulatory and litigation risks, and be costly to defend.

As a bank director, you need to be engaged in overseeing your bank's fair lending compliance efforts. That does not mean that you need to learn all of the technical details of the fair lending laws, but you should have a basic understanding of them, as well as an understanding of the role of the board of directors in overseeing your bank's efforts to comply with those laws.

That is the objective of this book.

As bank directors with many responsibilities, we know that you may not have the time to read this book in its entirety. However, while we strongly recommend that you read at least Chapters I and II, someone on your board or in management should read the book in its entirety and be in a position to address issues raised in the book with the board or a board committee. We also strongly recommend that your chief compliance officer and fair lending officer read the entire book.

What Is Fair Lending?

With the enactment of the Fair Housing Act in 1968 and the Equal Credit Opportunity Act in 1974, Congress declared lending discrimination illegal in the United States. The term "fair lending" was not defined by statute, however, until enactment of the Dodd-Frank Wall Street Reform and Consumer Protection Act of 2010 ("Dodd-Frank Act"). Under the Dodd-Frank Act, fair lending means "fair, equitable, and nondiscriminatory access to credit for consumers."[1]

1

The purpose of the fair lending laws is to prevent discrimination in lending on certain prohibited bases, as explained later in this book. Fair lending differs from, but is complementary to, responsible lending, which conceptually concerns economic and procedural fairness and transparency in dealing with consumers.[2]

What Are the Primary Federal Fair Lending Laws?

There are two primary federal fair lending laws. The Equal Credit Opportunity Act ("the ECOA"), which is implemented by Regulation B, prohibits discrimination in any kind of extensions of credit for consumer and business purposes. The Fair Housing Act ("FHAct"), which is implemented by regulations of the U.S. Department of Housing and Urban Development ("HUD"), prohibits discrimination in residential real estate-related transactions, including mortgage loans.

Both the ECOA and the FHAct have five prohibited bases in common – race, national origin, color, religion, and sex (including sexual orientation and gender identity) – but each have unique additional prohibited bases.

The ECOA also prohibits creditors from discriminating against credit applicants on the basis of marital status, age, receipt of public assistance income, or because of a consumer's good faith exercise of any right under the Consumer Credit Protection Act. In addition, the FHAct prohibits discrimination based on handicap (disability) and familial status (defined as children under the age of 18 living with a parent or legal custodian, pregnant persons, and people securing custody of children under 18).

This book will refer to the prohibited bases under the ECOA and the FHAct collectively as "protected classes." More background on these laws can be found in Appendix A. The states also have enacted anti-discrimination laws, some of which are modeled after the federal laws, but others that are much broader in their scope.

What Does a Fair Lending Allegation Look Like?

Fair lending enforcement actions and lawsuits allege unfavorable treatment of an applicant or a borrower on a prohibited basis (*e.g.*, race, ethnicity, gender, age, national origin) in some aspect of a credit transaction.

The ECOA applies to both consumer and business credit products, including mortgage loans, credit cards, auto loans, student loans, and other non-mortgage loan products. All types of credit products are covered by the ECOA.

The FHAct applies to "residential real estate-related transactions," which includes mortgage lending for first and second liens. It does not apply to non-mortgage credit products.

Because the ECOA and the FHAct both apply to mortgage lending, plaintiffs or regulators often cite violations of both laws when bringing lawsuits or enforcement actions related to alleged discrimination in mortgage lending.

Most public enforcement activity under the fair lending laws concerns underwriting and pricing of credit products, but the scope of the fair lending laws is actually much broader. Fair lending obligations apply to all aspects of a bank's credit-related activities for the entire life cycle of a product, including product development, advertising and marketing, taking and processing applications, underwriting, pricing, servicing, collections, loss mitigation, repossession, and foreclosure.

Why Fair Lending Should Be Among Your Bank's Top Compliance Priorities

Federal government agencies with fair lending supervisory and enforcement authority have become increasingly active in pursuing efforts to enforce the federal fair lending laws through their supervision, examination, and enforcement activities, resulting in numerous public and non-public settlements. Since its inception in 2011, the Consumer Financial Protection Bureau ("CFPB" or "Bureau") has generally considered fair lending enforcement one of its top priorities, and, during the Obama and Biden administrations, the CFPB has taken aggressive actions in supervision, examinations and enforcement actions to enforce those laws. The U.S. Department of Justice ("DOJ") has also vigorously enforced the federal fair lending laws since the early 1990's and entered into numerous consent orders with lenders (often jointly with the CFPB) to settle allegations of discrimination. The DOJ reported that, in 2014 alone, it oversaw the distribution of over $500 million to consumers in connection with fair lending settlements dating back to 2010.[3]

One of the most unique aspects of the federal fair lending laws is that the CFPB and the federal banking agencies (Federal Deposit Insurance Corporation ("FDIC"), Office of the Comptroller of the Currency ("OCC") and Federal Reserve Board ("FRB")) are required under the ECOA to refer matters to the DOJ for investigation when they have reason to believe a lender has engaged in a "pattern or practice" of discrimination. Referrals are also made under the ECOA by the FTC, and under the FHAct by HUD. No other federal consumer protection law has this feature. When the DOJ receives a referral from a federal agency, it determines whether to open an investigation or return the matter to the regulator for administrative enforcement. However, the DOJ also has authority to enforce the ECOA and the FHAct on its own initiative.

From 2001 through 2020, the CFPB, federal banking agencies, the FTC and HUD referred a total of 489 matters involving a potential pattern or practice of lending discrimination to the DOJ, and 158 of those referrals involved alleged discrimination on the basis of race or national origin.[4] Needless to say, a referral to the DOJ for a pattern or practice of discrimination poses high reputational and regulatory risk.

Unprecedented Enforcement Actions in the Mortgage Industry

Since 2010, federal agencies have required several major banks to enter into the largest mortgage fair lending settlements in history.

4

For example, in December 2011, the DOJ entered into its largest fair lending settlement ever — totaling approximately $335 million — to resolve allegations that Countrywide Financial Corporation discriminated against African American and Hispanic borrowers by charging higher fees and interest rates on residential mortgage loans, as well as steering such borrowers into subprime mortgages from, 2004 to 2008.[5]

In July 2012, the DOJ announced its second largest fair lending settlement — totaling approximately $175 million — in a case involving Wells Fargo Bank with similar mortgage pricing discrimination allegations.[6]

In October 2021, the federal regulators also announced an "all of government" effort to combat redlining, which is the practice of a mortgage lender failing to make an adequate amount of mortgage loans in areas with majority-minority populations.[7] Two recent examples of these redlining cases involved multi-million dollar settlements with the DOJ, OCC and the CFPB.[8]

Significant Enforcement Actions for Auto and Other Non-Mortgage Credit

Sizable fair lending settlements have also occurred in non-mortgage lending contexts.

To illustrate, in December 2013, the CFPB and the DOJ entered into consent orders with Ally Bank and Ally Financial (together, "Ally") requiring Ally to pay $80 million in damages to presumed African American, Hispanic, and Asian/Pacific Islander borrowers who allegedly paid higher dealer mark-ups on their auto loans than presumed white non-Hispanic borrowers, as well as $18 million in civil money penalties.[9] Dealer mark-up is the amount by which an auto dealer may mark up the interest rate above an indirect auto lender's risk-based buy rate based on the lender's discretionary pricing policy.[10] The CFPB and the DOJ subsequently entered into similar settlements with American Honda Finance Co., Fifth Third Bank, and Toyota Motor Credit Corporation during the period from 2014 through 2016 on the basis that their dealer discretionary mark-up policies allegedly led to discrimination against protected class borrowers who paid higher interest rates than white non-Hispanic borrowers with comparable credit profiles.

In June 2014, the DOJ and the CFPB entered into the federal government's largest credit card discrimination settlement in history — totaling $169 million — to resolve allegations that Synchrony Bank, formerly known as GE Capital Retail Bank, denied Hispanic borrowers the opportunity to participate in credit card debt repayment programs by excluding from its direct mail campaign customers with a mailing address in Puerto Rico and customers who requested to receive communications in Spanish.[11]

In 2017, the CFPB entered into a consent order with American Express alleging that the bank used different credit standards and collection practices in Puerto Rico, as compared to the mainland United States, and the consent order involved the payment of $96 million in consumer redress, almost all of which had been paid by the bank prior to the consent order.[12]

Fair Lending Must Be a Key Regulatory Focus for Banks of All Sizes

Experience has proven that regional or community banks are no better insulated from fair lending enforcement actions than large national retail banks.

To illustrate, in September 2012, Luther Burbank Savings, which had $3.7 billion in assets at that time, entered into a settlement with the DOJ for $2 million to resolve allegations that the bank's $400,000 minimum residential mortgage loan amount policy adversely impacted African American and Hispanic borrowers, and residents of majority-minority census tracts throughout California.[13]

In March 2013, Community First Bank, a $7 million bank based in Pikesville, Maryland, entered into a settlement with the OCC to resolve a rare reverse discrimination claim.[14] The OCC alleged that Community First Bank's mortgage lending

6

program, which provided lender credits to women and minorities, resulted in more costly loans to the bank's white and married borrowers. Under this settlement, the bank was required to pay $73,000 in restitution to 64 borrowers.

Private Fair Lending Litigation Is Alive and Well

Private plaintiffs and consumer advocacy organizations have also actively pursued fair lending claims by filing administrative complaints with federal government agencies and individual lawsuits and class actions against banks.

For example, in *Ramirez v. Greenpoint Mortgage Funding, Inc.*,[15] three minority consumers in California who had obtained mortgage loans from GreenPoint successfully brought a class action on behalf of other Hispanic and African American borrowers alleging that GreenPoint violated the federal fair lending laws because its discretionary pricing policy led to a higher likelihood of loan officers charging protected class borrowers disproportionately high rates, points, and fees, and increased the average cost of mortgage loans to minorities. GreenPoint resolved the allegations by paying $14.7 million to harmed borrowers in 2011.

In addition, the National Fair Housing Alliance ("NFHA") has conducted investigations relating to the maintenance and marketing practices of real estate owned ("REO") properties owned by several lenders and servicers in major metropolitan cities nationwide.[16] Based on the findings of these investigations, NFHA filed jointly with HUD complaints against several banks and Fannie Mae on the basis that their REO properties in minority communities were not maintained and marketed in the same manner as properties located in majority white areas.

The first of these complaints was filed against Wells Fargo in April 2012. In June 2013, HUD and Wells Fargo entered into a conciliation agreement, which required the bank to improve its REO marketing and maintenance practices and to invest $39 million in 45 communities through programs designed to support home ownership, neighborhood

7

stabilization, property rehabilitation, and housing development.[17] In May 2015, NFHA announced that, after a five-year investigation, it had filed with HUD a housing discrimination complaint against Fannie Mae for "wreaking havoc on middle- and working-class communities of color nationwide through a pattern of neglect . . . ."[18]

NFHA has filed complaints predicated on similar REO marketing and maintenance claims against Bank of America, Deutsche Bank, and a number of Fannie Mae's service providers.[19]

Furthermore, several municipalities have initiated fair lending lawsuits against mortgage originators and secondary market participants. These cases typically involve allegations that a lender steered minority borrowers into unfavorable or subprime loans, which in turn caused an increase in foreclosures. Other cases involve allegations that lenders failed to adequately provide credit to residents of predominantly minority communities. Due to the resultant rise in foreclosures, municipalities contend that they were economically harmed in several respects, including via lower property values, reduced tax revenues, and the increased demand for health and safety services. Municipalities that have recently filed such lawsuits include Miami and Miami Gardens, Florida; Los Angeles and Oakland, California; and certain counties in both Georgia and Illinois.[20]

Emerging Fair Lending Issues

The interpretation of fair lending laws is just beginning with respect to new practices that entered the financial services marketplace in recent years. Regulators are expressing concern about how machine learning underwriting models can carry "algorithmic bias,"[21] and are also grappling with the issue of creditors' use of non-traditional, or "alternative" data in underwriting decisions.[22] Another emerging issue is the use of consumers' demographic information – including protected characteristics like race, ethnicity and gender – to target advertisements on social media or internet platforms for credit products.[23] These areas are just beginning to receive attention, so it is important to follow developments in these areas as they unfold and ensure that your institution is responding to those developments.

Risks of Non-Compliance

The risks of non-compliance with the federal fair lending laws are significant, including regulatory risk, reputational risk, operational risk, and legal risk from lawsuits. Under the current regulatory and enforcement environment, violations of the fair lending laws and regulations may result in more frequent examinations, downgrades of a bank's compliance and/or Community Reinvestment Act examination ratings, and restrictions on a bank's ability to open new branches and engage in mergers or acquisitions, thus potentially prohibiting banks from executing their strategic plans.

Why Every Bank Director Should Read This Handbook

As a member of the board of directors, you are responsible for providing oversight of your bank's fair lending compliance program. In addition to understanding the federal fair lending laws and regulations and recent enforcement trends, regulators will also expect you to be knowledgeable about where fair lending risks exist within your bank. You should understand how and where fair lending risk may arise in your bank's various lending channels and its controls and processes for identifying and addressing fair lending risk. This information should be provided to the board through periodic updates from compliance management and perhaps third-party consultants or legal counsel, depending on the topic.

The *AABD Practical Handbook on Fair Lending for Bank Directors and Executive Officers* ("Handbook") is intended to provide members of the American Association of Bank Directors and other bank directors and CEOs with practical tips on how to provide adequate oversight of fair lending risk across their institution. Fair Lending Officers and/or other compliance professionals will also find best practices identified in the

Handbook that can be used to enhance their bank's fair lending compliance program.

The Handbook serves as a primer on key federal fair lending laws and highlights recent developments in fair lending enforcement and litigation. The Handbook is not intended to provide legal advice or serve as a comprehensive treatise on fair lending. For fair lending legal advice, we recommend that you consult legal counsel.

Fair lending requirements have evolved from being rules-based — where specific actions are mandated or prohibited — to principles-based, where industry, regulatory, and public interpretations have contributed to setting fair lending compliance expectations and best practices.

As interpreted by the regulators, fair lending obligations are far-reaching and somewhat unpredictable. As a result of these regulatory expectations, fair lending risk management imposes significant compliance burdens upon financial institutions of all sizes. It is important to note, however, that each bank must manage its own fair lending risks; fair lending risk management cannot be outsourced to a third party. Moreover, buyers in the secondary market are not insulated from fair lending risk simply because they did not originate the loan.

Given the government's vigorous supervision and enforcement of fair lending laws and regulations, as well as evolving regulatory expectations, even the most seasoned bank director should read this Handbook (or, at the very least, Chapters I and II with a designated director or member of management reading it in its entirety and reporting to the board). A bank that falls back on yesterday's tried-and-true techniques of managing fair lending risk will fall short of meeting today's regulatory expectations. This new world of fair lending compliance requires bank directors and CEOs to view all aspects of their institution's lending activities through a more critical lens.

CHAPTER II.   YOUR ROLE IN OVERSEEING FAIR LENDING RISK

Regulators expect that a bank's board of directors will play a key role in providing oversight of their institution's fair lending program, which requires hiring competent fair lending risk management staff, providing appropriate resources and budget for the fair lending program, and setting clear expectations concerning the importance of fair lending practices within the bank. This Chapter discusses regulatory expectations for bank directors, and provides guidance on how directors can work to meet those expectations.

A.   Board and Management Oversight

To effectively oversee fair lending risk, the board of directors should be generally knowledgeable about the fair lending laws and regulations. As a threshold matter, board members should receive foundational fair lending training from their institution, followed by annual fair lending training focused on new fair lending regulatory developments and emerging areas of risk. This book also serves as a way for board members to become more knowledgeable about fair lending laws and practices.

It is important to understand that there are two primary federal fair lending laws:

- The **Equal Credit Opportunity Act** ("the ECOA") makes it unlawful for any creditor to discriminate against an applicant on a prohibited basis during any aspect of a credit transaction. A creditor also cannot make any oral or written statement, in advertising or otherwise, to applicants or prospective applicants that would discourage on a prohibited basis a reasonable person from making or pursuing an application. The ECOA applies to both consumer and commercial credit. The ECOA also applies to the entire credit life cycle, including product development, advertising, marketing, originations,

11

servicing, collections, and foreclosure or repossession.

- The **Fair Housing Act** ("FHAct") makes it unlawful to discriminate in any aspect of the sale, rental, or financing of a dwelling (known as a "residential real estate-related transaction") on a prohibited basis.

There are also several key federal laws that support the objectives of the federal fair lending laws or complement those laws but are not fair lending laws *per se*:

- The **Community Reinvestment Act** ("CRA") was enacted to require banks to provide credit to residents of low- and moderate-income neighborhoods in their local communities, consistent with safe and sound banking practices.

- The **Home Mortgage Disclosure Act** ("HMDA") requires certain mortgage lenders to collect and report to federal regulators, and disclose to the public, certain data about mortgage loan applications and originations, including the race, national origin, and gender of loan applicants.

- Responsible lending laws include Section 5 of the Federal Trade Commission Act, which prohibits **unfair or deceptive acts and practices** ("UDAP"), and Sections 1031 and 1036 of the Dodd-Frank Act, which prohibits **unfair, deceptive, or abusive acts or practices** ("UDAAP").

Appendix A contains more detailed information on each of these laws, including a complete listing of the prohibited bases under the ECOA and the FHAct. Appendix B contains a list of related regulatory guidance and examination procedures.

Typically, a fair lending officer or chief compliance officer is responsible for managing a bank's fair lending program, which includes reporting elevated risks up to management and the board, where appropriate. As a bank director, you are responsible for providing oversight for your bank's fair lending program, together with the rest of the board, or a board committee, if authority is delegated to a board committee. Depending on the size of the bank, at least one management-level compliance risk committee may exist to provide in-depth oversight of the bank's fair lending program. Larger banks may have two or more risk committees that are responsible for managing and addressing fair lending risk.

Both the board of directors (or its delegated committee) and the bank's compliance risk management committee should review and approve the institution's fair lending policy annually, receive copies or summaries of fair lending audit and examination findings, and receive periodic fair lending risk management reports. The latter reports may include fair lending risk assessment results, a report on the state of the fair lending program, statistical analysis results (particularly where disparities are detected and remediation is recommended), and reports on fair lending complaints. Receiving this information on a regular basis will allow the board and any assigned committees to objectively gauge how their bank is managing its fair lending risk and to detect any "red flags" for fair lending risk (discussed further in Chapter V).

Fair lending reports should be appropriately calibrated so that the board of directors receives the most critical information that it needs to know in a form that is high-level, yet meaningful and clear, whereas compliance risk management committees should receive more in-depth reports that allow the committee to review detailed information and data.

Regulators frequently evaluate board and board committee minutes to ensure that directors are actively engaged in fair lending oversight. Therefore, board minutes, as well as board committee minutes, should reflect any dialogue at the meetings about reports included in the board or board committee packet.

B.   Asking the Right Questions

To understand your bank's fair lending risks and controls, you should review the results from your bank's fair lending risk assessment. Regulators typically expect such risk assessments to be performed annually. Fair lending risk assessments are critical to understand areas of heightened risk within your bank and serve as a tool for the legal or compliance team to establish and/or adjust the fair lending monitoring and testing schedule each year.

To fully appreciate a bank's fair lending risk, it is important for directors to ask the right questions when engaging in a dialogue with compliance and legal staff. Below are some common questions that may be appropriate for you to ask to assess your bank's fair lending risk:

Questions for Bank Directors to Assess Fair Lending Risk
• Where do the greatest fair lending risks lie within our bank?
• What controls do we have in place to manage those risks?
• Are those controls formalized in policies and procedures or more of a business practice?
• Are those controls automated or manual?
• Are those controls tested periodically to ensure that they are working properly? If so, what are the results of those tests? Who receives the results from that testing within our bank?
• To what degree does our bank allow the use of discretion by underwriters, loan officers, or third parties (e.g., mortgage brokers or auto dealers) in underwriting or pricing? Does our bank have controls in place to manage the use of discretion?

- How does our bank manage credit and pricing exceptions?

- Does our bank limit those exceptions to a certain percentage of loan volume (e.g., 10 to 20%)?

- Are exception reports generated and are they reviewed by compliance for potential fair lending risk?

- How does our bank evaluate fair lending risk for new or modified loan products and policies?

- What processes and controls does the bank employ concerning third parties that originate loans for the bank?

- Has our bank evaluated fair lending risk in loan servicing activities (known as "fair servicing risk")?

- What controls does the bank have in place to ensure that consistent levels of service are provided to customers?

- Have there been any recent examinations or compliance department or audit findings concerning our bank's non-compliance with fair lending laws and regulations?

- What are some best practices that our bank's peers are doing to manage their fair lending risk that our bank is not doing?

- Has our bank received any consumer complaints alleging discrimination or unfair treatment? If so, have those complaints been properly reviewed by legal and compliance staff to understand whether the allegations are credible and whether the bank needs to take any corrective action? Do such complaints reveal any trends?

- Have any fair lending complaints led to litigation or regulatory involvement?

- What do you believe are emerging fair lending issues that our bank should be concerned about?

These types of questions will demonstrate to management and regulators that you understand the importance of controlling the bank's fair lending risk and helping establish a culture of compliance in this critical area.

C.   Hiring or Developing a Fair Lending Officer

In today's regulatory environment, banks should strongly consider having a fair lending officer on staff to manage the bank's fair lending program, work with the business unit management to identify and address fair lending risks, and interface with regulators. Depending on the size, scope, and complexity of your bank's products/services and its geographic lending footprint, you may not have a dedicated fair lending officer. Instead, a compliance officer may wear more than one hat and manage compliance for multiple areas.

Although the ideal fair lending officer candidate should already have fair lending compliance risk management experience, fair lending officers are in high demand by banks and even non-banks subject to fair lending laws. As a result, qualified candidates are often difficult to find and recruit. Therefore, some banks may need to consider developing an internal or external candidate with some compliance experience through mentoring.

If seeking a qualified candidate externally, it may be a good idea to hire a professional search firm that specializes in finding compliance professionals across the U.S. Ideally, fair lending officer candidates should have an undergraduate degree, at least five years of experience in compliance risk management, prior experience as a fair lending officer, and experience in interacting with, and making presentations to, executive management and regulators.

While it is preferable to look for a fair lending officer candidate who already has fair lending compliance risk management experience, if an individual has a fairly extensive background in compliance generally, he or she could likely transition into a role as a fair lending officer with adequate guidance and mentoring. It may be appropriate to have a less seasoned fair lending professional begin as a fair lending manager until they develop more expertise in the area.

If a qualified external candidate cannot be found, then one option is to develop an internal candidate to become a fair lending officer. Banks often take one of two approaches: (i) developing a candidate who is already a member of the compliance risk management group (usually a compliance manager), or (ii) grooming a business manager who has extensive knowledge of lending products and/or underwriting and pricing practices.

Development of either an external or internal candidate may take place by having the chief compliance officer and/or in-house fair lending attorney (or outside counsel) mentor the individual and teach him or her fair lending concepts and risks. The individual also should learn the business on an in-depth basis — particularly underwriting, pricing, and loss mitigation practices — for both mortgage and non-mortgage products.

Sometimes when neither an appropriate internal nor external candidate can be found to assume the role of fair lending officer, a bank may choose to table the search for a period of time and instead engage an experienced compliance consultant to serve as the fair lending officer on a temporary basis (e.g., 3 to 6 months). Although this approach can be costly, it addresses the need to immediately fill the role while moving the fair lending program forward until the right candidate can be found.

D. Fair Lending Program Resources

Once a fair lending officer is in place, it will be critical to ensure that he or she has an appropriate team, tools, budget, and resources to support the program. Regulators expect the board of directors to ensure that appropriate staffing and resources are provided for the fair lending program, which should be commensurate with the size, complexity, and risk profile of the institution. Periodically, fair lending program resources should be revisited to ensure that they continue to meet the institution's needs.

E. Integration of Responsible Lending Concepts into Fair Lending Programs

Over the past decade, many financial institutions have expanded their existing fair lending programs by incorporating responsible lending and responsible banking concepts to reflect an increasing emphasis by regulators, the media, consumer advocacy groups, and consumers themselves on responsible lending/banking practices. Responsible lending/banking requires compliance with several laws, including UDAP and UDAAP, and focuses on equitable treatment of, and transparency toward, consumers by providing full disclosure and informed choice to consumers. Responsible lending is viewed as a concept that is highly complementary to fair lending, so regulators view combined fair and responsible lending programs favorably. Today, these integrated compliance risk management programs are typically known as "fair lending and responsible banking" programs.

In light of these developments and as you oversee your bank's fair lending program in your role as a bank director, you should consider whether it may be appropriate to expand the scope of your institution's program to include responsible lending/banking concepts to keep pace with regulatory expectations.

CHAPTER III. WHAT TYPES OF LENDING DISCRIMINATION VIOLATE THE FAIR LENDING LAWS?

Courts have recognized three legal theories under which government agencies and plaintiffs may bring cases alleging discrimination under the federal fair lending laws.

A. Legal Theories of Lending Discrimination

1. Overt Discrimination

Overt discrimination occurs when a lender openly and intentionally discriminates against an applicant or a borrower on a prohibited basis. Overt discrimination may include written policies or procedures. For example, if a lender has a policy where it offers a credit card with a limit of up to $750 for applicants aged 21 to 30 and $1,500 for applicants over 30, this policy would likely be viewed as discriminatory based on age. Overt discrimination may also include oral statements where a lender expresses a discriminatory preference, even if the lender does not act upon this preference. For instance, overt discrimination on the basis of sex (gender) occurs if a loan officer states that the bank prefers not to make loans to women unless their spouses co-sign the loan. In the fair lending arena, overt discrimination is relatively uncommon.

2. Disparate Treatment

Disparate treatment occurs when a lender treats an applicant or a borrower differently on a prohibited basis. This standard does not require any evidence that the treatment was motivated by prejudice or that the lender intended to discriminate against a particular class of persons. Disparate treatment can occur simply by treating similarly situated people differently on a prohibited basis without a legitimate, nondiscriminatory reason for that difference in treatment.

To illustrate, disparate treatment occurs when a loan officer processes loan applications for non-minority applicants immediately, but informs minority loan applicants that it would take several days to process an application. The most common disparate treatment cases arise from allegations of pricing or denial disparities that are unfavorable to borrowers in a protected class group compared to similarly situated white non-Hispanic borrowers.

Disparate treatment may be established through direct or circumstantial evidence that a creditor used a prohibited characteristic in making a credit decision. If a plaintiff provides direct evidence that a credit decision was based on a prohibited factor, then the creditor must prove that it would have made the same credit decision even if it had not considered the prohibited factor.

To prove disparate treatment using circumstantial evidence, plaintiffs generally must establish that they are a member of a protected class, were rejected for a credit product despite being qualified for it, and that the creditor continued to approve credit for similarly situated applicants. Once these factors are established by the plaintiff, the burden shifts to the creditor to state a legitimate, non-discriminatory reason for the adverse action. Finally, the burden shifts back to the plaintiff to show that the legitimate reason for the adverse action was merely a pretext for discrimination.

3. Disparate Impact

Disparate impact occurs when a lender applies a facially neutral policy or a practice equally to all applicants or borrowers, but the policy or practice has a disproportionately negative effect on members of a protected class. To prove disparate impact, there is no need to demonstrate that the lender intended to discriminate.

For example, regulators take the position that a policy establishing a minimum loan amount for single family home mortgages may disproportionately affect minority purchasers, who may have lower incomes or wish to buy homes in areas with lower property values, thus resulting in disparate impact.[24] Under the disparate impact theory of discrimination, the plaintiff is not required to establish intent and, therefore, it is irrelevant whether the bank actually intended to discriminate on a prohibited basis. Courts have traditionally applied a three-step, burden-shifting test to determine whether a defendant can be found liable under the fair lending laws for discrimination under a disparate impact test.

First, the plaintiff must allege that the lender's neutral policy or practice, when applied equally to all credit applicants, disproportionately excludes or burdens a protected class of applicants on a prohibited basis, resulting in disparate impact. This is typically demonstrated through statistical evidence. Second, the lender must refute this allegation by demonstrating that the policy or practice is justified by business necessity. This is often known as "business justification," and relevant factors may include cost, competition, and profitability, among others. In the third step, even if the lender can show a business justification or necessity, the practice may still be found to be in violation if an alternative policy/practice could serve the same purpose with less discriminatory effect on members of a protected class.

a.   HUD's disparate impact rulemaking

HUD's attempt to codify the agency's standards for disparate impact claims brought under the FHAct, which occurred over a 10-year period from 2013 through 2023, is a long saga punctuated with lawsuits, judicial stays, a U.S. Supreme Court case that played a prominent role in shaping the history of the rule, and three rulemakings by the agency.

HUD amended its 2013 disparate impact regulation in October 2020 to better reflect the U.S. Supreme Court's 2015 ruling in *Texas Department of Housing & Community Affairs v. Inclusive Communities*, which held that a defendant may be liable under the FHAct for a policy or practice that has an adverse impact on members of a protected class group.[25] Although the rule was supposed to go into effect in October 2020, a federal court enjoined its implementation and in June 2021, HUD published a proposal to rescind the 2020 disparate impact rule and replace it with the original 2013 rule. HUD finally issued its final rule on March 31, 2023 reinstating its 2013 rule.[26] *See* Appendix A for more detailed information.

The Supreme Court's decision in *Inclusive Communities* and HUD's re-adoption of its 2013 disparate impact rule is expected to embolden government agencies and private plaintiffs to continue to assert claims of disparate impact discrimination under the FHAct and the ECOA. Therefore, it is advisable for banks to examine new and existing policies, procedures, and business practices for the potential risk of disparate impact and take steps to reduce fair lending risk. This may include modifying or discontinuing the policy or practice, or reaching a satisfactory conclusion that the policy/practice does not in fact cause disparate impact by using the Supreme Court's approach to the three-step test.

B.   Types of Lending Discrimination

Within the three theories of fair lending claims (overt discrimination, disparate treatment, and disparate impact), there are different types of lending discrimination that can be raised by a regulator or plaintiff. Examples include allegations of redlining, reverse redlining, and steering.

1.   Redlining

What Is Redlining?

Redlining occurs when a bank refuses to extend credit or provides unequal access to credit in certain neighborhoods because of the race, ethnicity, national origin, or other protected characteristic of its residents. There has been a steady stream of redlining cases brought by the DOJ since 1994, with no sign of slowing down. Significantly, in October 2021, the DOJ announced a comprehensive and unprecedented "Combatting Redlining Initiative" which seeks to partner with U.S. Attorney's Offices, State Attorneys General, and financial regulatory agencies by taking a "whole of government" approach to enforce the federal fair lending laws. The initiative also seeks to expand the DOJ's analyses of potential redlining to both depository and non-depository institutions.[27] Examples are discussed below.

Examples: Redlining Enforcement Actions

In September 2022, the DOJ entered into a $13 million settlement with Lakeland Bank to resolve allegations that it engaged in redlining by avoiding providing loans to prospective applicants and engaging in conduct that would discourage applications from prospective applicants in majority-Black and Hispanic census tracts in the Newark, New Jersey, metropolitan area.[28]

In July 2022, the DOJ and the CFPB entered into a $22 million settlement with Trident Mortgage Company ("Trident") to resolve allegations that Trident redlined majority-minority neighborhoods through its marketing, sales, and hiring practices. This is the first resolution of redlining allegations involving a nonbank mortgage lender by the DOJ and the second largest redlining settlement in the agency's history.[29]

In June 2016, the DOJ and CFPB entered into a $10.6 million settlement with BancorpSouth Bank to resolve allegations that it engaged in illegally redlining in Memphis, Tennessee by allegedly placing its branches outside of minority neighborhoods, excluding minority neighborhoods from the area it chose to serve under the Community Reinvestment Act, and directing its marketing away from minority neighborhoods.[30]

Traditionally, regulators have evaluated redlining risk by reviewing a bank's Community Reinvestment Act ("CRA") assessment area. Heightened redlining risk was indicated if a bank's main office and/or branches operated in or around historically racially segregated cities or if a bank chose to close a branch in an area with a high proportion of minority residents without reasonable business justification. Although banks should continue to ensure that their CRA assessment areas do not exclude any geographic areas with higher concentrations of minority residents and evaluate their branch opening/closing strategy in such areas, regulators are defining redlining risk quite differently in recent years. Importantly, a bank's various entry points into the market must demonstrate diversity. Some of the new triggers for redlining risk include the following:

- Lack of marketing and advertising in minority media
- Lack of products that tend to be more appealing to residents of census tracts with a majority of minorities (known as "majority-minority" census tracts)
- Geographic placement of loan officers in primarily non-minority census tract locations
- Geographic placement of third-party loan referral sources, such as brokers and real estate agents
- Lack of loan officers focused on CRA lending

Regulators are also looking at applying disparate impact theories in redlining allegations — in particular, whether a bank's policies or procedures may cause a disparate impact of not lending to minorities in certain geographic areas.

As noted in the list of redlining risk triggers above, regulators are now extending redlining risk to lenders that engage only in wholesale lending. Increasingly, there appears to be a regulatory expectation that such lenders will seek out brokers to penetrate majority-minority census tracts by obtaining loans from minority borrowers and that wholesale lenders will make other affirmative efforts to penetrate those markets.

Example: Redlining Enforcement Actions – An Area of Focus for State Regulators

The State of New York has been very active in investigating and bringing enforcement actions concerning alleged redlining activities. In September 2015, the New York Attorney General ("NYAG") entered into a $825,000 settlement with Evans Bank, N.A. and Evans Bancorp, Inc., a regional bank that the NYAG alleged failed to offer mortgage products to residents of predominantly African American neighborhoods

24

in Buffalo, New York.[31] In the press release announcing the lawsuit, the NYAG stated that this case was part of ongoing investigations by the NYAG into potential redlining activities across the state.[32] In February 2021, the New York State Department of Financial Services subsequently released a report regarding its inquiry into redlining in Buffalo, New York.[33]

2. Reverse Redlining

What Is Reverse Redlining?

Reverse redlining occurs when a lender intentionally targets the marketing of certain products or services with less favorable terms, conditions, and/or pricing toward a particular group on a prohibited basis, such as race, ethnicity, or national origin. In recent years, several municipalities filed cases against residential mortgage lenders based on reverse redlining allegations that they targeted minority communities for subprime loans, and that defaults on those loans led to foreclosures and vacancies, which in turn resulted in increased municipal costs and decreased property tax revenues.[34]

Examples: Reverse Redlining Enforcement Actions

In June 2022, the DOJ entered into a $4.5 million settlement agreement with Advocate Law Groups of Florida, P.A. ("ALG") to resolve allegations that ALG targeted Hispanic homeowners for predatory mortgage loan modifications.[35]

In February 2015, the DOJ, together with the U.S. Attorney's Office for the Western District of North Carolina and the North Carolina Department of Justice, announced a settlement of the DOJ's first discrimination lawsuit involving "buy here, pay here" auto lending.[36] The $225,000 settlement resolved allegations that two North Carolina-based used car dealerships, among other things, engaged in reverse redlining by intentionally targeting African American customers for predatory car loans. The settlement requires substantial reforms to the dealerships' lending and servicing practices.

3.   Steering

What Is Steering?

Steering involves promoting different programs within a loan type (*e.g.*, prime versus subprime auto loans) with less favorable terms, conditions, or pricing to otherwise qualified borrowers in a way that treats them differently on a prohibited basis.

Example: Steering Lawsuit

In 2015, the City of Oakland, California, sued Wells Fargo, alleging that Wells Fargo engaged in discriminatory lending in violation of the FHAct by steering minority borrowers into mortgages with unfavorable terms and higher costs.[37] Oakland asserted that Wells Fargo's practices resulted in it giving minority borrowers a higher proportion of riskier adjustable-rate loans than to white borrowers and fewer conventional 30-year fixed rate mortgages to minority borrowers. Oakland alleged that these lending practices led to increased foreclosures and reduced tax revenue. After winding its way up and down the courts for several years, the Ninth Circuit Court of Appeals ultimately dismissed the lawsuit in 2021.

In February 2015, the Fair Housing Justice Center, a New York City-based fair housing non-profit organization, filed a lawsuit against one of the top 20 largest banks in the U.S. alleging that the bank's loan officers in New York City (i) used neighborhood racial demographics to steer minorities to racially segregated neighborhoods and (ii) steered prospective buyers to mortgage loan products with different terms and conditions based on race and national origin.[38] The organization hired nine female "testers" of varying racial and ethnic backgrounds who acted as first-time homebuyers who were married and without children. The organization alleged that the bank's loan officers encouraged minority testers to apply for loan programs that were limited to homes located in majority-minority neighborhoods or in low-to-moderate income areas, and discouraged white testers from doing so. The organization also alleged that the bank favored white applicants during the prequalification process. For instance, it was alleged that a more qualified Hispanic tester was told that she would qualify for a mortgage $125,000 less than what a white tester could obtain. The parties settled in September 2015.[39]

CHAPTER IV.   WHERE DOES FAIR LENDING RISK LIE?

Although regulators have traditionally focused on lending areas that permit human judgment (*e.g.*, underwriting and pricing), fair lending requirements apply to all aspects of credit-related lending and servicing activities across the loan life cycle, which include:

- New product development
- Advertising and marketing
- Taking and processing credit applications
- Loan origination - Underwriting and pricing
- Servicing
- Collections
- Loss mitigation and loan modifications
- Repossession and foreclosure
- REO property maintenance

Fair lending obligations apply to all consumer and commercial credit products, including but not limited to mortgage loans, auto loans, unsecured loans, credit cards, student loans, overdraft protection, and small business loans. This Chapter discusses some of the key sources of risk in the consumer credit administration process and product-specific considerations.

It's important to note that fair lending risk may arise well before a prospective customer actually applies for credit. In particular, front-line staff and loan officers should be trained to provide fair and consistent service to all prospective customers to avoid discouraging credit applications, which is prohibited by the ECOA and Regulation B. In addition, fair lending implications should be considered when developing strategies regarding where a bank will establish branches, which products it will develop or offer, and to whom and where the bank will target in its product advertising and marketing efforts. As a bank director, you will want to ask about fair lending training for customer-facing staff and whether your bank's branching, new product development, or marketing strategies may create possible redlining, reverse redlining, or steering risk.

A.   New Product Development

It is critical to ensure that any new lending products or services are developed, implemented, and maintained in a manner that complies with fair and responsible lending laws. To that end, it is important that legal and compliance representatives have a seat at the table as new products or services are being discussed and designed, and then are part of the review and approval process as new products and/or services are implemented.

Although the board of directors has responsibility for product development oversight, the new product and service review and approval process is typically executed through a new product development committee or managed through an appropriate compliance risk management committee that includes representatives from legal and compliance on the committee. Alternatively, it may involve *ad hoc*, product-specific meetings with written sign-off required on the new initiative by legal and/or compliance representatives. Regardless of the internal process chosen, it is imperative to demonstrate that compliance with fair lending laws was considered and addressed as part of the new product and service development and implementation process.

B.   Advertising and Marketing

The two federal fair lending laws — the ECOA and the FHAct — each contain provisions related to non-discriminatory advertising and marketing for extensions of credit. For example, under the ECOA and Regulation B, creditors may not directly or indirectly engage in any advertising or marketing to applicants or prospective applicants that would discourage (or selectively encourage), on a prohibited basis, a reasonable person from making or pursuing an application for credit. Specifically, a bank cannot either expressly state or imply a preference for, or exclusion of, any customers on a prohibited basis. The ECOA does not prohibit creditors from distinguishing and treating higher-risk applicants differently than lower-risk applicants, regardless of the applicants' membership in any protected class.[40]

30

Under the fair lending laws, banks must also ensure that any marketing response models or other methods used to identify or select the recipients of advertising or promotional materials comply with applicable fair and responsible lending laws.

Where required by the FHAct and HUD's implementing regulations, advertising and marketing materials in connection with mortgage lending activities must include a facsimile of the equal housing lender logo and the phrase "Equal Housing Lender" or a statement to the effect that the bank makes housing loans without regard to an applicant's prohibited basis characteristics.

As a best practice, it is a good idea to require preapproval from legal and/or compliance prior to using any advertising or marketing materials. This approach helps ensure that any advertising and marketing materials comply with applicable laws, including the fair lending laws. Compliance with responsible lending laws such as UDAAP should also be considered as part of the review by legal and compliance of any advertising and marketing materials.

Example: Marketing Models Matter

In June 2014, the CFPB and the DOJ announced parallel enforcement actions — totaling $169 million — against Synchrony Bank, formerly known as GE Capital Retail Bank, based on allegations that the bank excluded 108,000 borrowers from credit card repayment programs who indicated that they preferred communications to be in Spanish or who had a mailing address in Puerto Rico, even if the customers met the promotion's qualifications. The CFPB and the DOJ asserted that as a result, Hispanic populations were unfairly denied the opportunity to benefit from certain promotions, and, as a result, Synchrony Bank violated the ECOA by discriminating against them on the basis of national origin and race.[41] The Synchrony Bank settlement reinforces the importance of considering fair lending implications in all aspects of a bank's marketing activities.

C. Credit Application Taking and the Prohibition on Discrimination and Discouragement of Prospective Applicants

It is critical that all customer-facing staff provide fair and consistent service to both prospective customers and existing customers when taking credit applications to avoid discouraging applicants, on a prohibited basis, from submitting a credit application. Discouragement of prospective credit applicants is prohibited by Regulation B, which implements the ECOA. Toward this end, all employees should be required to take fair lending training that discusses both the anti-discrimination and anti-discouragement aspects of the ECOA and Regulation B on at least an annual basis.

Example: Discouragement of Prospective Credit Applicants Found

In October 2021, the CFPB and the DOJ, in cooperation with the OCC, brought a redlining enforcement action against Trustmark National Bank ("Trustmark") alleging that from 2014 through 2018, Trustmark avoided providing home loans and other mortgage services and discouraged applications for credit for properties in majority-Black and Hispanic neighborhoods in the Memphis, Tennessee-Mississippi-Arkansas Metropolitan Statistical Area.[42]

In the complaint, the Bureau alleged that the location of Trustmark's branches and its marketing practices resulted in discouraging residents of majority-Black or Hispanic neighborhoods from applying for credit. Specifically, Trustmark maintained only four of its 25 branches in majority-Black or Hispanic neighborhoods, which resulted in discouraging the residents of majority-Black or Hispanic neighborhoods from applying for credit. Of the four branches in majority-Black or Hispanic neighborhoods, only three were full-service branches and two of the branches were established or acquired at a time when the surrounding neighborhoods were majority-white. The Bureau also found that from 2001 through 2018, Trustmark established four new branches, three of which are located in majority-white neighborhoods.

Additionally, the Bureau alleged that Trustmark did not assign any mortgage loan officers to its branches located in majority-Black and Hispanic neighborhoods. Trustmark relied on its mortgage loan officers to develop referral sources, conduct outreach to potential customers, and distribute marketing materials, but the bank did not supplement their efforts to generate mortgage loan applications from majority-Black and Hispanic areas. Further, the Bureau alleged that Trustmark marketed through print and digital advertising that were primarily distributed in majority-white neighborhoods.

Ultimately, Trustmark, the CFPB and the DOJ entered into a consent order which required Trustmark to pay $3.85 million into a loan subsidy program for majority-Black and Hispanic neighborhoods, increase its presence in those areas, pay a $5 million civil money penalty, and implement proper fair lending procedures.

Example: Case Alleging Discouragement of Prospective Credit Applicants Dismissed

In July 2020, the CFPB filed a lawsuit against Townstone Financial, Inc. ("Townstone"), a Chicago mortgage lender, for alleged redlining practices. The Bureau specifically alleged that Townstone had violated the ECOA by discouraging prospective African American applicants in the Chicago metropolitan area from applying for mortgage loans through its marketing practices.[43]

In the complaint, the CFPB alleged that from 2014 through 2017, Townstone's HMDA data showed that the company drew around 2,700 applicants, only 37 (1.4%) of which came from African Americans in the Chicago metropolitan area. During that same period, it drew only five or six applications (0.8%) each year from majority-African American neighborhoods even though such neighborhoods make up 13.8% of the census tracts. While Townstone allegedly drew between 1.3% and 2.3% of its applications from properties in majority-African American neighborhoods, from 2014 through 2017, its peers drew many times more (between 7.6% and 8.2%). The CFPB alleged that Townstone's acts, including derogatory comments made about African American neighborhoods on its podcast, discouraged prospective African American applicants from applying for mortgage loans. The Bureau argued that Regulation B extends the ECOA's prohibition to discouraging "potential applicants."

Townstone moved to dismiss, arguing the suit was an attempt by the CFPB to expand the reach of the ECOA to "prospective applicants," when the statute itself only prohibits discrimination against "applicants." The district court agreed with Townstone, noting that the word 'applicant' is used 26 times in the ECOA, and the statute does not prohibit or discuss conduct prior to the filing of an application. The court found that because the text of the ECOA is unambiguous, it owed no deference to the regulatory definition of "applicant" found in Regulation B. It therefore held, "[t]he CFPB cannot regulate outside the bounds of the ECOA," and dismissed the case in February 2023.

D.   Loan Origination

1.   Mortgage Lending

For the past 30 years, mortgage fair lending regulatory examinations, investigations, and enforcement actions have traditionally focused on the use of discretion in the judgmental underwriting and pricing process where insufficient controls were found to mitigate the risk of discrimination. After the Great Recession of 2008, federal regulators continued to pursue such investigations and enforcement actions with a renewed emphasis on access to credit and eliminating pricing disparities for protected class groups compared to white non-Hispanic applicants.

Example: Discriminatory Underwriting and Pricing

On July 25, 2016, the CFPB and the DOJ brought a joint action against BancorpSouth Bank ("BancorpSouth") alleging that the bank denied certain African Americans home mortgage loans more often than similarly situated non-Hispanic white applicants, charged African American customers more for certain mortgage loans than non-Hispanic white borrowers with similar credit profiles, and implemented an explicitly discriminatory loan denial policy.[44]

Specifically, the CFPB found that BancorpSouth granted employees in its Community Banking Department substantial discretion in decisioning home mortgage loan applications and that its General Loan Policy provided only minimal guidance on how borrower or loan characteristics should affect the underwriting decision. Loan officers were also not required to document how borrower or loan characteristics influenced their decisions. The Bureau conducted a fair lending statistical regression analysis and found that African Americans were denied loans substantially more often than similarly situated white applicants.

The Bureau also found that the Community Banking Department charged African American borrowers higher mortgage loan rates than white borrowers and that loan officers had "nearly unfettered discretion" to set the price of the mortgage loans. BancorpSouth did not have a process in place to ensure loan officers priced loans consistently and did not require loan officers to document the factors they considered in making their decision. The Bureau conducted a statistical regression analysis and found that the pricing disparities between African American and white borrowers was statistically significant.

Notably, the CFPB alleged that BancorpSouth's Mortgage Department implemented a policy or practice that required employees to treat applicants differently based on race, color, national origin, or other prohibited characteristic. Specifically, loan officers were instructed to turn down minority applicants more quickly than white applicants and not provide credit assistance to borderline applicants. The CFPB supported this allegation with an audio recording of an internal meeting that clearly articulated the Bank's policy or practice of rejecting minority applicants more quickly. In that meeting, a manager instructed employees under her supervision to turn down minority applicants within 21 days and turn down borderline applicants quickly, while white applicants were not subject to this shorter review period. Following the manager's articulation of this race-based policy, the recording documents employees making derisive comments about minorities.

Under the terms of the Consent Order, BancorpSouth was required to pay $4 million in direct loan subsidies in minority neighborhoods in Memphis; invest at least $800,000 in community programs, advertising, outreach, and credit repair; pay $2.78 million in restitution to African American consumers who were unlawfully denied or overcharged for loans; pay a $3 million civil penalty; and submit a pricing and underwriting compliance plan that included policies and procedures that are designed to ensure consistent application of objective underwriting and pricing criteria and to avoid unlawful discrimination.[45]

Examples: Discretionary Pricing

Discretionary pricing has often been the focus of regulatory enforcement actions, even more so than underwriting practices to approve or deny a mortgage application. In December 2013, the DOJ and the CFPB entered into a key $35 million settlement with PNC Bank, as successor-in-interest to National City Bank, to resolve discriminatory pricing allegations.[46] The allegations were based on pricing disparities for African American and Hispanic borrowers as low as nine basis points. Therefore, pricing disparities of less than 10 basis points are now enough to result in a referral to the DOJ from the CFPB or one of the prudential regulators. In 2013, the DOJ also entered into settlements based on discriminatory pricing allegations with Chevy Chase Bank and Southport Bank, which required consumer restitution of $2.85 million and $687,000, respectively.[47]

Pricing disparities are not restricted to the annual percentage rate and may instead focus on a disparity in fees, even if there is no allegation that the overall cost of the loan was higher.[48] For example, the DOJ entered into a $6.1 million settlement with AIG Federal Savings Bank in 2010 to resolve allegations that it allowed wholesale mortgage brokers to charge African American borrowers higher upfront broker fees than to white borrowers from 2003 to 2006.[49]

Example: Underwriting Discrimination

Regulators have also sharpened their focus on the underwriting practices of certain mortgage lenders to determine if they had illegally denied any applicants' mortgages, or refinancings of mortgages, based on sex, familial status, or disability because the borrower was pregnant or on parental leave. Beginning in July 2010, HUD issued a series of enforcement actions against mortgage lenders and mortgage insurers alleging discrimination against pregnant borrowers and those on parental leave.

To illustrate, on July 1, 2014, HUD announced a conciliation agreement with Greenlight Financial Services ("Greenlight") to resolve allegations that it violated the FHAct when it denied or delayed processing of mortgage loans to women because they were on maternity leave.[50] The conciliation agreement was driven by a complaint from a married couple alleging that Greenlight denied their refinancing application because the wife was on maternity leave. HUD's investigation revealed that Greenlight also allegedly denied four other applicants who were on maternity leave, or delayed their applications until after the women returned to work. The agreement required that Greenlight pay $20,000 to the couple who filed the complaint, and $7,000 to each of the other four applicants identified by HUD.

a.   Redlining discrimination

In recent years and particularly under the Biden administration, the DOJ, CFPB, and prudential regulators have been focused on addressing and eradicating redlining practices, which are illegal under both the ECOA and the FHAct. In October 2021, the DOJ (together with the CFPB and OCC) announced a comprehensive and unprecedented "Combatting Redlining Initiative" in which it sought to partner with U.S. attorneys, state attorneys general, and financial regulatory agencies by taking a "whole of government" approach to enforcing the federal fair lending laws.[51] Since the launch of this initiative, the DOJ has announced four redlining consent orders with record settlements and a combined $75 million in relief, with many more investigations underway.

Most of the redlining enforcement actions undertaken by the DOJ and the CFPB follow a familiar "playbook" alleging that the bank discriminated against racial and ethnic minorities based on the geographical area in which they reside by failing to engage in marketing outreach and/or provide sufficient banking products and services, and then requiring a set of remedies to address redlining allegations. Such remedies typically include modifying fair lending compliance programs to analyze redlining risk; enhanced fair lending training for staff; hiring of additional mortgage loan officers in minority neighborhoods; significant investments in loan subsidy funds, community development, and marketing outreach; and establishment of at least one branch in the redlined neighborhood. We expect that redlining investigations and enforcement actions will continue to be a large focal point of the DOJ's and CFPB's work.

Example: Redlining Discrimination

In September 2022, the DOJ entered into a $13 million settlement with Lakeland Bank ("Lakeland") to resolve allegations that it engaged in redlining by avoiding providing loans to prospective applicants and engaging in conduct that would discourage applications from prospective applicants in majority-Black and Hispanic census tracts in the Newark, New Jersey, metropolitan area. The consent order provides that Lakeland will invest $12 million in a loan subsidy fund for residents of Black and Hispanic neighborhoods in the Newark area; spend $750,000 for advertising, outreach, and consumer education; and invest $400,000 for development of community partnerships to provide services that increase access to residential mortgage credit. In addition, Lakeland must open two new branches in neighborhoods of color and employ four mortgage loan officers and a Community Development Officer to serve neighborhoods of color in the Newark area. This settlement represents the third largest redlining settlement in DOJ's history.

2.   Auto Lending

Indirect auto lending was a key priority for the CFPB's fair lending supervisory and enforcement work from 2013 through 2018, during which period the Bureau issued fair lending guidance to the industry and undertook numerous investigations and enforcement actions against indirect auto lenders, as more fully described below.

Under the Obama administration, the CFPB issued a controversial fair lending auto finance bulletin in 2013 that provided general guidance with respect to fair lending compliance and the indirect auto lending industry.[52] In that bulletin, the Bureau contended that by permitting dealer mark-up and compensating dealers on that discretionary basis, lenders may be liable under the legal theories of both disparate treatment and disparate impact when pricing disparities on prohibited bases exist within their portfolios.[53] The CFPB took the position that dealer mark-up and compensation policies are alone sufficient to trigger lender liability. The CFPB also suggested that lenders should either eliminate dealer pricing discretion or be required to establish a comprehensive fair lending program to mitigate the risk of discretionary dealer mark-up. Then in September 2014, the Bureau released additional guidance on its plans to supervise and enforce auto lenders' compliance with consumer finance laws, including fair lending laws.[54]

From 2013 through 2016, the CFPB actively pursued multiple pricing disparity investigations and enforcement actions against auto lenders and auto finance companies. In December 2013, the CFPB and the DOJ announced their first joint fair lending enforcement action against an indirect auto finance company to resolve allegations that Ally Bank's and Ally Financial's dealer compensation policy, which allowed for auto dealer discretion in pricing, resulted in disparate impact upon certain minority borrowers.[55] At that time, the $98 million settlement was the DOJ's third largest fair lending enforcement action ever. The CFPB subsequently entered into large settlements with three other indirect auto lenders – American Honda Finance Corporation ($24 million),[56] Fifth Third Bank ($18 million),[57] and Toyota Motor Credit Corporation ($21.9 million)[58] – during the period 2015-2016.

With the CFPB's guidance on indirect auto lending and the Ally Bank settlement, indirect auto lenders were put on notice of the Bureau's regulatory expectation to impose sufficient controls or revise dealer mark-up and compensation policies, implement a strong fair lending compliance and monitoring program, and address risks through monitoring and corrective action programs.

In 2018, however, Congress used its authority under the Congressional Review Act[59] to require the CFPB to rescind its auto finance/fair lending bulletin based on overreaching by the Bureau, and that action largely curtailed the CFPB's auto finance enforcement activities during the Trump administration. Afterward, the CFPB did not publicly pursue auto finance pricing disparity issues, and even abandoned active matters it was pursuing in supervision and enforcement.

However, the CFPB now appears to be re-engaging in responsible lending enforcement in the auto finance space. For example, on January 4, 2023, the CFPB and the New York Attorney General sued Credit Acceptance Corporation, a major subprime auto lender, for alleged predatory lending practices by mispresenting the cost of credit, engaging in aggressive debt collection tactics, and violating New York usury limits and other consumer financial protection laws.[60]

Recently, the New York Department of Financial Services ("The NYDFS"), known for being an aggressive state regulator, has begun to bring pricing disparity cases against New York-chartered banks that engage in indirect auto lending.

During the period 2021 through 2022, the NYDFS entered into settlements with three indirect auto lenders, in which the agency alleged pricing disparities that adversely impacted racial/ethnic protected class groups.[61] Specifically, the NYDFS alleged that, as a result of disparate impact caused by the lenders' pricing policies, racial and ethnic minorities were charged a higher average dealer mark-up than non-Hispanic white borrowers. The NYDFS required each bank to pay civil penalties, make restitution to borrowers, and implement remedial measures. To our knowledge, this is the first time a state regulator has pursued fair lending dealer mark-up charges against an assignee of retail installment sales contracts and could foreshadow similar actions by other state regulators.

As a result of these developments at both the federal and state levels, fair lending regulatory and reputational risk in the auto finance sector is increasing and will likely remain heightened.

3. Unsecured Lending

Since its inception in 2011, the CFPB has been gathering information on so-called payday and other short-term lending products. The CFPB has expressed concerns that certain forms of short-term loans are "debt traps" and cautioned that the agency would exercise its authority to best protect consumers while preserving access to responsible credit.[62] Prudential regulators, namely the FDIC and the FRB, have also referred matters involving unsecured consumer loans to the DOJ since 2011.

Fair lending risk in unsecured lending may arise in several contexts, including marketing, origination, product usage, payment processing, collection practices, and third-party relationships. In particular, marketing materials and sales tactics should be evaluated to ensure that payday and other short-term lending products are not being targeted to protected class borrowers. Although race and ethnicity data are limited for non-mortgage credit, some studies have suggested that protected classes comprise a larger percentage of the payday loan borrower population. For example, a 2012 Pew Charitable

Trusts study on payday lending indicates that the odds of payday loan usage are 105% higher for African Americans compared to other races and minorities.[63]

The CFPB has brought multiple enforcement actions against lenders that offer payday lending-type products, as well as pawnbrokers, alleging UDAAP violations for the way in which the product was marketed and sold and often alleging that the lender engaged in aggressive debt collection tactics despite knowing that customer delinquency and default was highly likely. *See, e.g.*, *In the Matter of ACE Cash Express*[64] (alleging, among other things, that a short-term lender entrapped customers in a so-called "cycle of debt" and engaged in aggressive collections practices); *In the Matter of EZCORP, Inc.*[65] (alleging, among other things, that a short-term lender engaged in aggressive payment and collection practices).

In the context of fair lending, the prudential regulators have referred unsecured lending matters involving potential fair lending "pattern or practice" violations to the DOJ. These matters are further discussed below.

Examples: Unsecured Lending Enforcement Actions
Originated by the Prudential Regulators

The DOJ's settlement with Nixon State Bank ("Nixon") in 2011 marked the agency's first pricing discrimination lawsuit involving unsecured consumer loans in more than 10 years.[66] Under the terms of that settlement, the bank was required to pay nearly $100,000, conduct employee fair lending training, and revise pricing policies that were alleged to have resulted in higher prices on unsecured loans made to Hispanic borrowers in violation of the ECOA.

And in 2013, the DOJ announced its $159,000 settlement with Fort Davis State Bank, which was also based on claims that the bank charged higher prices for unsecured consumer loans to Hispanic borrowers in a discriminatory manner.[67]

Nixon and *Fort Davis State Bank* arose from examinations conducted by the FDIC in 2010 and 2011, respectively. For both cases, it is noteworthy that the DOJ claimed that loan officers were given broad discretion in the origination and pricing process, which in turn led to a disparate impact on Hispanic borrowers.

In January 2015, the DOJ announced a $140,000 settlement with First United Bank, predicated on similar claims. *First United Bank* was also referred to the DOJ by the FDIC.[68]

a.   CFPB's Payday Lending Rule

While not directly related to fair lending, the CFPB and consumer advocates have long criticized financial institutions offering short-term loans for their failure to consider the consumer's "ability to repay." This criticism, after years of "studies" and deliberation, ultimately developed into the CFPB's misleadingly named rule on "payday, vehicle title, and certain high-cost installment loans" (which may apply not only to 0% APR loans but longer-term loans with large principal amounts made to high-net worth individuals). The rule was initially promulgated in November 2017 and imposed underwriting/ability to repay and payment-related requirements on "covered loans." The underwriting/ability to repay requirements were ultimately rescinded as of November 19, 2020 after a change in leadership at the CFPB.

Currently, the rule covers, with some exceptions, (a) loans with terms of 45 days or less; (b) certain loans with a term in excess of 45 days (i) that are repayable in a single payment, (ii) that have a scheduled payment that is twice the size of another scheduled payment, or (iii) that do not fully amortize and have a final payment that is twice as large as any prior installment payment; <u>and</u> (c) certain loans with APRs in excess of 36% where the lender obtains an "autopay" or similar payment authorization.

The remaining payment provisions regulate how "covered lenders" may collect payments on covered loans. The core of the rule is a "two consecutive strikes and you're out" provision under which a lender may not continue to initiate payments (e.g., via ACH or payment card under an "autopay" arrangement) if two consecutive lender-initiated payments are returned unpaid. Once there are two consecutive returns, the lender must obtain a new authorization from the consumer before re-starting an autopay arrangement. The rule also requires lenders to provide a number of payment-related notices to consumers (e.g., information on upcoming and failed payments).

While the CFPB's final rule technically became "effective" in August of 2019, this date has been stayed by industry-led litigation that the U.S. Supreme Court is currently considering for certiorari after the Fifth Circuit found the rule (and the entire structure of the CFPB) to be unconstitutional.

Regardless of whether the CFPB rule actually becomes effective, the CFPB's current leadership has committed to explore additional mechanisms and pursue what it views as its core concepts in the rule (i.e., the mandatory underwriting provisions) through other means such as examination and enforcement. In that vein, we are aware that the CFPB has issued enforcement and/or civil investigative demands to multiple small dollar lenders in the context of the borrower's ability to repay. However, it is currently unclear whether these CFPB actions are primarily aimed at payday lending or rather all forms of high-APR/small dollar lending, but the initial salvo arguably is broad enough to encompass the latter.

4.   Credit Cards

Regulators have identified several areas of fair lending risk when offering credit cards — from marketing strategies to underwriting and ancillary products to rewards programs for high-net worth clientele. For example, in August 2014, the Federal Reserve Bank of Philadelphia released a discussion paper titled *Fair Lending Analysis of Credit Cards*,[69] which addresses fair lending risks in various stages of the marketing, acquisition, and management of credit card accounts.

One month later, an FRB economist published an article titled, "Race, Ethnicity, and Credit Card Marketing,"[70] which examines the relationship between race, ethnicity, and the probability that a borrower would receive a credit card offer — via a direct mail solicitation — from one of five top credit card issuers. The article reported that even after controlling for credit history, household income, and local economic conditions, Black borrowers were 27% less likely to receive a credit card offer, and Hispanic borrowers were 17% less likely to receive a credit card offer. This article underscores the importance of marketing in providing equal access to credit.

Example: Discriminatory Credit Card Activities

Since its inception in 2011, the CFPB has undertaken three key fair lending enforcement actions against credit card issuers. As an illustration, in October 2012, the CFPB announced an enforcement action against three American Express subsidiaries for violating consumer protection laws from every stage of the consumer experience, from marketing to enrollment to payment to debt collection.[71] Specifically, the Bureau alleged that American Express subsidiaries (i) deceived consumers who signed up for the American Express "Blue Sky" credit card program by leading them to believe they would receive $300 in addition to bonus points for signing up, but not providing all qualified consumers with the $300; (ii) charging unlawful late fees; (iii) unlawfully discriminating against new account applicants on the basis of age through its use of a credit scoring system that treated charge card applicants differently on the basis of age; (iv) failing to report consumer disputes to consumer reporting agencies; and (v) misleading consumers about debt collection by leading consumers to believe that there were benefits to paying off old debt.

The Joint Consent Order among the CFPB, FDIC and American Express required American Express to take the following actions: cease the alleged illegal practices related to marketing, late fees, credit reporting and age discrimination; pay an estimated $85 million in restitution to approximately 250,000 consumers; implement new procedures to ensure

45

compliance with consumer financial protection laws; and pay a civil monetary fine of $18 million, which consisted of $14.1 million to the CFPB and $3.9 million to the FDIC. The press release noted that Synchrony also paid separate civil monetary fines of $9 million to the FRB and $500,000 to the OCC.[72] Therefore, American Express paid total civil money penalties of $27.5 million to resolve this matter with the Bureau and the prudential regulators.

In credit card channels, a bank should review underwriting and pricing practices (including scorecards, pricing exceptions, and credit policy overrides) for fair lending compliance. Credit line increases and decreases should also be conducted in a fair and consistent manner.

Advertising and marketing strategies and materials must be reviewed for fair lending compliance and appropriately reflect diversity. In particular, regulators have become increasingly concerned with a credit card provider's target or suppression marketing criteria. Banks should closely review marketing campaigns that exclude certain marketing segments to ensure that these exclusions are not based on protected class characteristics. Many credit card providers offer special benefits, terms, or products to its premier or high-net worth customers. These programs and products in particular should be reviewed for potential fair lending risk. It is also important to ensure that clear, consistent, and nondiscriminatory criteria for your bank's programs and products are well documented.

5. Student Lending

Student loans have surpassed credit cards as the largest source of unsecured consumer debt. As outstanding balances have grown and defaults have risen, the Biden administration has taken steps to try to reduce student loan debt and even try to cancel such debt for certain borrowers.

Since its inception in 2011, the CFPB has made student lending a priority and has taken several steps to implement and expand its oversight of student lenders. Fair lending compliance in student lending is now a new area of regulatory scrutiny by the CFPB, the DOJ and prudential regulators.[73]

Credit and pricing models that use non-credit bureau attributes are particularly susceptible to regulatory scrutiny. These attributes include cohort default rates ("CDRs"), graduation rates, retention rates, and whether a school is a for-profit/not-for-profit or a two-year/four-year institution. For example, the CFPB's examination guidelines require that examiners determine whether the lender uses CDRs as part of its student loan eligibility criteria and evaluate the entity's justification for using this attribute in credit decisioning and pricing.[74] CDRs are a measure of the federal student loan repayment history of a particular group or "cohort" of borrowers, which often based on the college or university the borrower attends. CDRs are often used by private student lenders as a proxy for a student's likelihood of repaying debt as part of underwriting and pricing decisions. This can pose fair lending concerns because racial and ethnic minority students are disproportionately concentrated in schools with higher CDRs.

A regulator may also scrutinize a bank's assessment of a student's future ability to pay. Typically, an ability-to-pay analysis in the student loan context is based on a student's major or future occupation, which may present fair lending concerns, particularly under the disparate impact theory. This is because certain protected classes may be over-represented in certain occupations. Teaching and nursing are two examples of traditionally female-dominated professions.

As with other credit products, marketing practices are also a key focal point for the regulators. The CFPB has examined how student borrowers are solicited and whether the lender has used different marketing efforts based on loan product (e.g., products for certain majors), schools, or geography.[75] In the servicing context, lenders should also ensure that borrowers are treated fairly and consistently in loan modifications, collections, and fee waivers.

6.   Overdraft Protection

Although regulatory compliance concerns for overdraft programs primarily involve UDAP or UDAAP issues — such as re-ordering checking account transactions in a manner that increases consumer cost, missing or confusing information, misleading marketing materials, and disproportionate impact on low-income and younger consumers — overdraft programs are also subject to the ECOA.

In 2005, the OCC, FRB, FDIC, and NCUA initially issued joint guidance on overdraft protection programs. In that guidance, the agencies stated that "steering or targeting certain consumers on a prohibited basis for overdraft protection programs while offering other consumers overdraft lines of credit or other more favorable credit products or overdraft services, will raise concerns under the ECOA."[76] In addition, the FDIC has issued guidance to clarify that a bank's "[i]nconsistent application of waivers of overdraft fees will be evaluated in light of fair lending statutes and regulations."[77] Therefore, it is important to review your institution's overdraft program for both responsible lending (UDAP/UDAAP) and fair lending concerns.

The CFPB has scrutinized overdraft fees for many years. In addition to bringing four enforcement actions against lenders for alleged violations of laws related to overdraft fees during the period from 2015 through 2020, the CFPB issued a Data Point report entitled *Overdraft/NSF Fee Reliance Since 2015 – Evidence from Bank Call Reports* (Dec. 1, 2021), in which the Bureau found that banks continue to heavily rely on overdraft and NSF revenue, which then made up two-thirds of reported bank fee revenue. In the press release accompanying that report, the CFPB stated that it would be "enhancing its supervisory and enforcement scrutiny of banks that are heavily dependent on overdraft and similar fees." CFPB Director Chopra further noted that the Bureau "will be taking action to restore meaningful competition to this market."

Despite the banking industry's trend toward either eliminating or reducing overdraft and NSF fees since 2020 (particularly by large and mid-size banks), the CFPB has continued a campaign against these fees. Among other things, the CFPB issued a request for information on "exploitive junk fees" (including overdraft and NSF fees) in January 2022 requesting public comments to help shape the Bureau's rulemaking, guidance and enforcement agenda.[78] In October 2022, the CFPB subsequently issued guidance on unfair practices concerning "surprise" overdraft fees.[79] In addition, the CFPB's Fall 2022 Rulemaking Agenda notes that the Bureau is considering rulemakings related to overdraft and NSF fees, which are listed as in the pre-rule stage.

E.   Servicing, Collections, and Loss Mitigation

Since the mortgage crisis in 2008, regulators have expected that financial institutions will engage in "fair servicing" activities by treating borrowers fairly, consistently, and objectively in the servicing, collections, loss mitigation, and foreclosure processes. Fair servicing concepts arise from the fact that the ECOA applies across the entire credit life cycle, and the FHAct prohibits discrimination against borrowers applying for mortgage loans, modifications, or repayment plans. Fair servicing issues most often occur in the context of delinquent and defaulted loans. To mitigate fair servicing risks, banks should develop controls to ensure the fair and consistent treatment of customers in credit line increases and decreases, account closures, fee waivers, collections, loss mitigation, and foreclosure.

F.   Maintenance of REO Properties

As discussed in the Introduction, the NFHA has initiated several lawsuits against banks, servicers, and third-party vendors involving claims that REO properties in minority communities were not maintained and marketed in the same manner as REO properties in majority white communities and alleging disparate treatment. The first of these lawsuits, which involved Wells Fargo, settled in June 2013.[80] The NFHA and HUD also initiated a lawsuit against Fannie Mae, one the nation's largest owners of foreclosed properties, based on similar claims.[81] See Chapter I for more information.

CHAPTER V. SPOTTING "RED FLAGS" FOR FAIR LENDING RISK

This Chapter identifies several common "red flags" for fair lending risk that you should be aware of so you can determine whether your bank is taking appropriate steps to identify, manage, and mitigate those risks.[82] As a bank director, it is important for you to keep a watchful eye out for these and other red flags as you review your bank's compliance reports and engage in discussions with your bank's legal and compliance staff concerning how fair lending risks are managed at your bank. Examples of other red flags are found in endnote 82.

Red Flag #1: Use of discretion in consumer lending

As we discussed in Chapter III, areas that allow discretion in the lending process attract regulatory scrutiny and increase fair lending risk. Policies and procedures often permit loan officers, underwriters, or third parties (*e.g.*, mortgage brokers or auto dealers) to exercise discretion in underwriting and pricing. Discretionary practices may also arise in account maintenance (*e.g.*, fee waivers), collections, loss mitigation, and loan modifications. Regulators specifically focus on these areas in which discretion is exercised by bank personnel in fair lending examinations to evaluate adequacy of controls and ongoing monitoring/testing.

If your bank allows employees discretion in the loan origination and/or servicing process, it is important to ensure that appropriate controls are in place, such as policies, procedures and training, and to perform ongoing monitoring and testing of the discretionary activity. Controls, monitoring, and testing help ensure that discretion is exercised consistently; if not, appropriate remedial action should then be taken so that the consumer is not harmed.

Red Flag #2: Lack of periodic fair lending risk assessments

As discussed further in Chapter VI, regulators expect that banks of all sizes will conduct periodic fair lending risk assessments of their products, services, delivery channels, and operations to evaluate the level of compliance with applicable fair lending laws and regulations. Not conducting such risk assessments may cause the regulators to do a more in-depth assessment during examinations and raise questions about a bank's commitment to fair lending compliance.

Fair lending risk assessments may be conducted based on your bank's qualitative measures, quantitative analysis, or a combination of both. The methodology for the risk assessment should be reviewed periodically to reflect changes to applicable laws and regulations, and your own bank's products, services or business practices. The results of the risk assessments should be used to ensure that proper controls are in place at your bank (especially for high-risk areas) and to help allocate your compliance staff, budget, and resources appropriately to higher risk areas.

Red Flag #3: Disparate impact that may not be readily apparent

Potential disparate impact is often difficult to detect, so it is important to proactively review your bank's policies, procedures, and practices to determine if a risk of disparate impact may exist. This may be done through qualitative reviews, quantitative reviews, or statistical analyses.

Chapter IX discusses the types of statistical analyses that a bank could perform to assess its level of fair lending risk. Your bank should also conduct a review of marketing, advertising, underwriting, pricing, servicing, collections and foreclosure or repossession policies and procedures to evaluate whether they could have a disproportionately adverse impact on a protected class. If there is a potential disparate impact, your bank should determine whether the level of risk merits performing a formal, documented disparate impact analysis. This would include a determination of whether an adequate business justification for the policy or procedure exists, and whether there is a less discriminatory alternative that could achieve the same results.

Your bank's legal and compliance representatives should also review the variables that go into models for underwriting, pricing, collections and loss mitigation for potential disparate impact prior to implementation of the model. To reduce fair lending risk, it is advisable to avoid use of any variables that mirror protected class groups under the fair lending laws, or close proxies for them, in developing models. Examples of such variables include surnames, language preference, demographic information derived from social media, and receipt of Social Security benefits. In addition, we recommend avoiding any variables that involve geographic factors smaller than a state, such as counties or zip codes, because such variables may potentially include or exclude areas with demonstrably higher percentages of minority group residents and thus may pose redlining or reverse redlining risk. Similar to the disparate impact analysis for policies and procedures, if the results of the review show that one or more variables poses a risk of disparate impact, then your bank should determine (i) whether to omit the variable(s) from the model, or (ii) whether there is a less discriminatory alternative that could achieve the same results, and if not, then document the business justification for retaining the variable(s) in the model.

Red Flag #4: Failure to evaluate fair lending risks and controls for non-mortgage loans

For non-mortgage loan products, the government has relied on proxy data to conduct quantitative analyses in the absence of any HMDA data to serve as the basis of a fair lending claim. For example, in 2014, the CFPB issued a white paper on the BISG proxy methodology it uses to analyze fair lending compliance for auto loans.[83] The CFPB's BISG proxy methodology is now in use by many financial institutions for non-mortgage products, including auto loans and credit cards. Depending on its non-mortgage loan volume and the level of risk, your bank can determine whether it is appropriate to perform proxy testing on non-mortgage products.

At a minimum, all banks should review their preventive and detective controls for their non-mortgage lending channels to determine whether proper controls are in place.

Red Flag #5: Lending policies that require a minimum loan amount

Underwriting guidelines that impose minimum loan amounts have been the subject of numerous fair lending complaints and settlements. This is due to the perception that minimum loan amounts may have a disparate impact on minority borrowers who are more likely to live in neighborhoods and communities with lower property values and, therefore, require lower loan amounts.

As a case in point, in 2012, the DOJ announced a $2 million settlement with Luther Burbank Savings ("Luther Burbank") for setting a minimum loan amount of $400,000 for its wholesale single-family residential mortgage lending program.[84] The DOJ alleged that from 2006 through 2010, the bank's policy resulted in very few mortgage loan originations to African American or Hispanic borrowers in the Los Angeles area or in majority-minority tracts throughout California. In the greater Los Angeles area, for example, only 5.8 percent of Luther Burbank's single-family residential mortgage loans were made to African American and Hispanic borrowers during this time period, compared to 31.8 percent of such loans made to African American and Hispanic borrowers by comparable lenders. The complaint alleges that Luther Burbank continued its $400,000 minimum loan amount policy despite its knowledge that its low level of lending to African American and Hispanic borrowers, and in majority-minority census tracts, was attributable to the policy.

This minimum loan amount principle applies to both mortgage and non-mortgage products, especially to the extent that the minimum loan amount makes a product inaccessible to members of a protected class. To understand your bank's fair lending risk in this area, legal and compliance staff should review your bank's lending policies and procedures to identify any minimum loan amounts.

54

Red Flag #6: Credit overlays to underwriting guidelines

Your bank should regularly monitor whether certain credit overlays to underwriting guidelines have a disproportionate adverse effect on members of a protected class. Some examples of credit overlays that should be scrutinized or monitored on a regular basis include: (a) higher minimum FICO scores for Federal Housing Administration loans than what is required by HUD; (b) requiring female applicants on maternity leave to return to work before closing a mortgage loan (even when the applicant satisfies the income requirements while she is on maternity leave); and (c) requiring applicants receiving permanent disability benefits from the Social Security Administration to provide proof of continuation of the disability with a letter from a physician attesting to the nature of the disability and the expected duration of the disability.

Red Flag #7: Consumer complaints alleging discrimination or unfair treatment

Consumer complaints alleging discrimination or unfair treatment may be an early indicator of fair lending risk and are a key area of focus for the CFPB and the prudential regulators in examinations and supervision. In fact, even one complaint may lead to a targeted fair lending examination, investigation or enforcement action.

Banks should identify, review, and promptly respond to any consumer complaints related to fair lending. Ideally, legal and/or compliance professionals should respond to any fair lending complaints rather than complaint management staff because of the sensitive nature of such complaints.

As discussed in Chapter VI, banks should establish a robust system for tracking and monitoring all consumer complaints, including fair lending complaints. Summaries analyzing the quantity, types, and root causes of complaints, as well as any complaint trends, should be regularly provided to the board of directors and risk management committees. If systemic issues are identified, they should be promptly addressed.

Red Flag #8: Adverse fair lending regulatory examination or audit reports

It is important to prepare well in advance for a fair lending examination by the CFPB or a federal banking agency to ensure that your bank produces all necessary information requested by the agency and quickly responds to examiner questions during the off-site and on-site portions of the examination. If any adverse findings are communicated by the agency in regulatory exam reports, the bank should act to address and resolve any identified issues or Matters Requiring Attention quickly and thoroughly. It is critical that violations of the fair lending laws are not repetitive or it will reflect poorly on the bank. In fact, the CFPB launched a "Repeat Offender Unit" in 2022 that is geared toward reviewing and monitoring primarily large institutions' compliance with examination reports and enforcement consent orders.

Similarly, the bank should adequately prepare for any internal or external audit that assesses compliance with the fair lending laws, technical compliance with Regulation B, and the bank's Fair Lending Policy. If any adverse audit findings occur, the bank should also act expeditiously to address and resolve them.

Red Flag #9: Correlation between CRA downgrades and deficient fair lending performance

As a board member or bank executive officer, it is important to understand the correlation between CRA examination rating downgrades and fair lending performance. If a bank's fair lending exam results in findings that the bank is alleged to have engaged in discriminatory or other illegal credit practices, the prudential regulator will frequently downgrade the bank's CRA rating. Similarly, if a bank's CRA rating is downgraded following the conclusion of a CRA examination, then the bank's fair lending examination will also likely reflect poor performance. Therefore, the two are correlated. As a result, it is important to ensure that your fair lending risk management program and controls are in order, or it may result in a CRA downgrade.

Red Flag #10: Statistical analysis reveals disparities in underwriting and/or pricing outcomes

Fair lending statistical analysis is the way in which more subtle forms of discrimination (disparate treatment or disparate impact) are revealed to the bank and its regulators. Bank management should ensure that periodic testing of mortgage and non-mortgage consumer lending products occurs to determine whether any disparities exist in credit decisioning and/or pricing between white non-Hispanic applicants and protected class group applicants. Depending upon volume, for mortgage loans, HMDA data generally should be analyzed quarterly or semiannually, as well as annually; for non-mortgage consumer lending, testing should occur at least annually. If the results are unclear, additional analyses or file review may be warranted.

The board of directors should be periodically informed about the testing results. Directors should pay close attention to the results and ask questions as needed to fully understand them. After all testing is completed and if any statistically significant results are found that could indicate potential discrimination, then the fair lending officer, legal counsel, and senior management should jointly determine whether any adjustments to policies, procedures or practices, employee training, or consumer remediation are necessary or advisable as a corrective action plan.

Red Flag #11: Fair lending enforcement and other regulatory developments

Your bank should regularly monitor headlines, press releases, and agency announcements from the CFPB, the DOJ, and state and federal banking agencies regarding fair lending enforcement matters and other regulatory developments. The bank should conduct an analysis to determine whether the activity that is the subject of the enforcement matter or development impacts your bank's operational or compliance risk and whether any adjustments in policies, procedures, or practices are warranted.

CHAPTER VI.   FAIR LENDING RISK MANAGEMENT – HOW STRONG IS YOUR BANK'S PROGRAM?

This Chapter provides an overview of the key components of an effective fair lending compliance or risk management program (known as a "fair lending program"). In designing or evaluating your bank's fair lending program, it is important to recognize that there is no "one size fits all" approach. Each bank must develop and implement its own fair lending program that is tailored to the bank's size, complexity, and risk profile. As previously discussed in Chapter II, your bank should also strongly consider incorporating responsible lending/banking concepts into its fair lending program to manage both fair lending and responsible banking risks, including UDAP and UDAAP.

A.   A Fair Lending Policy Is Critical

A comprehensive, enterprise-wide fair lending policy is key to establishing a corporate culture that is focused on the fair and equitable treatment of consumers throughout the product life cycle. A fair lending policy that is reviewed and approved by the board of directors at least annually can demonstrate a bank's commitment to providing a "top down" approach to managing fair lending risk that starts with sound board and management oversight. A fair lending policy also serves to form the framework of your bank's fair lending program.

B.   Fair Lending Program Elements

1.   Risk Assessment

A fair lending risk assessment should be conducted at least annually by compliance management or qualified third parties across all businesses and products to understand the areas of risk within your bank across the entire loan life cycle. The board of directors should review a summary of the results of the risk assessment, focusing on the gaps between the risks and controls. The risk assessment is designed to qualitatively and/or quantitatively evaluate inherent fair lending risk, the adequacy of the control environment, and any residual fair lending risk.

The fair lending risk assessment may employ a methodology that consists of a review of relevant policies, procedures, and documentation; conducting interviews with key business, compliance, legal, and lending personnel concerning their knowledge of fair lending risks and any control gaps; reviewing quantitative fair lending analyses; and summarizing and validating each component of the review with appropriate personnel. A bank's risk assessment process should be tailored to the bank's size, complexity, and products and services offered. If possible, fair lending risk assessments should be performed at the direction of legal counsel to preserve the bank's attorney-client privilege of sensitive information.

2. Preventive Controls

In addition to a fair lending policy, a bank should have policies and procedures that describe how fair lending compliance is achieved at all stages of the bank's lending and servicing activities. Typically, this involves integrating fair lending concepts into key policies and procedures such as credit risk policies, pricing policies, underwriting procedures, and loss mitigation policies and procedures. Such policies and procedures should clearly allocate fair lending risk management responsibilities at all levels of the organization. Furthermore, ongoing monitoring should be performed to ensure that these policies and procedures are carried out in practice. Fair lending-related policies and procedures should be reviewed at least annually by the board of directors or management, as appropriate, and enhanced for areas that are likely to be subject to regulatory scrutiny such as pricing, credit risk and underwriting, fees, customer disclosures, marketing and advertising, loss mitigation, loan modification, and foreclosure and repossession.

Preventive controls should also include annual fair lending training for all employees involved in the loan origination and servicing process, as well as management and the board of directors. Job-specific fair lending training should

60

also be required based on the employee's job function, particularly if the role involves the exercise of judgment (*e.g.*, underwriters). Training should also be used to communicate any new fair lending-related legislative and regulatory changes.

Incentive compensation plans may also pose fair lending risk if they incentivize undesirable behavior (*e.g.*, product steering). Therefore, legal and compliance personnel should review incentive compensation plans for sales, underwriting, and servicing personnel at least annually to ensure that incentives are aligned with the fair lending laws. The board of directors also may approve incentive compensation plans– generally on an annual basis.

3.   Detective Controls

Detective controls (monitoring and testing) are an important component of a bank's fair lending risk management program because they help determine whether the bank's preventive controls are working or are otherwise adequate to manage fair lending risk. Detective controls include conducting ongoing monitoring and testing of automated, manual, or process-oriented controls designed to manage the use of discretion to ensure that they are effective and working as intended.

Statistical analyses and comparative file reviews (discussed in Chapter IX) may also be conducted to compare similarly qualified applicants and borrowers and ensure that any dissimilar treatment among protected and non-protected class groups is not related to a prohibited basis in relation to the levels of assistance provided, credit decisions made, and terms and pricing granted. Any fair lending testing and monitoring should be performed on an ongoing basis in order to monitor trends and identify areas of potential regulatory scrutiny. Management-level and board risk committees should receive periodic summaries of the results as appropriate to understand areas of heightened fair lending risk.

4.   Issue Identification and Corrective Action

If a potential fair lending issue is identified, it is important that the bank has a procedure for addressing and resolving the issue — and escalating it to management and the board of directors, if necessary. If a fair lending matter is escalated, management, the board of directors, or a board committee may make a decision, direct corrective action, or require further study of the matter.

A bank should maintain an issue tracking system and develop corrective action plans to ensure that each issue is resolved in a timely and appropriate manner. On a periodic basis, the status of any significant fair lending issue under management should be reported to appropriate risk committees and, if needed, to the board of directors.

5.   Reporting to Risk Management Committees

A bank's fair lending policy and program documentation should document an escalation and reporting process to ensure that executive management (and the board of directors, where necessary) is promptly alerted to any material issues involving fair lending non-compliance. On a periodic basis, ideally monthly or quarterly, the fair lending officer or chief compliance officer should report any significant fair lending developments to executive management and appropriate risk management committees.

6.   Consumer Complaint Management

Consumer complaints are a key area of focus for the CFPB and the prudential regulators. In fact, even one complaint may lead to a targeted examination, investigation or enforcement action. Banks should develop and maintain a robust consumer complaint management program to ensure that any fair lending complaints are properly identified, promptly responded to, and monitored or escalated, if needed. Fair lending complaints are typically reviewed and responded to by legal and/or compliance rather than the business line because of the heightened risk associated with allegations of discrimination.

To meet regulatory expectations, banks should establish a centralized system for tracking and monitoring consumer complaints (including fair lending complaints) and create periodic reports for the board of directors and any risk management committees that analyze complaint numbers, types of complaints, root causes, and trends. The board of directors should note any changes in volume and/or trends and, if needed, direct management to review policies, procedures, or practices and make any modifications necessary to address any systemic issues from an operational perspective.

7.   Periodic Internal Audits

On a periodic basis (such as annually), a bank should conduct an independent audit assessing its compliance with fair lending laws and regulations. The board and audit or other board committee may be involved in setting the scope of the fair lending audit and choosing the party to conduct the audit. The audit may be conducted by either internal audit or an external auditor, but most often the internal audit group conducts fair lending audits.

The internal audit group is typically asked to audit for compliance with the fair lending policy or conduct an audit of the fair lending program to ensure that it does not create any non-attorney/client privileged materials regarding fair lending. Because of the sensitivity, confidentiality, and complexity of fair lending statistical analysis, it is important that internal audit not conduct any statistical analyses of its own or evaluate fair lending regression models or results as part of the audit process.

The results from the fair lending audit should be shared with the board of directors, its audit committee, and appropriate management-level risk committees. The board and its audit committee should review the results of the audit and follow up if the results require corrective action.

CHAPTER VII.   EFFECTIVELY PREPARING FOR AND MANAGING A FAIR LENDING EXAMINATION

Banks of all sizes are subject to various types of examinations by federal and/or state regulators. Regulators use fair lending examinations to determine whether a bank is meeting its compliance responsibilities under federal or state fair lending laws and regulations. As a bank director, you are not expected to participate in the day-to-day aspects of your bank's examination process. Nonetheless, you should be familiar with the process because many fair lending enforcement actions have originated from fair lending examination findings. This Chapter discusses how a bank can effectively prepare for and manage a fair lending examination conducted by a federal regulator.

Depending on your bank's size and charter, the federal fair lending examination may be conducted by the CFPB or your bank's prudential regulator. Like other types of examinations, fair lending investigations and examinations typically consist of three primary components: (1) off-site analysis and review of information and data; (2) on-site examination of the bank's lending practices, policies and procedures, risk assessments, and reports; and (3) the written examination report.

Regardless of which federal regulator conducts your bank's fair lending examination, the key to a successful outcome to any bank examination is careful planning, preparation, and effective regulatory relationship management.[85] Below we provide some practical guidance on what to expect in a fair lending examination by your prudential regulator or the CFPB, and what your bank can do before, during, and after an on-site fair lending examination to ensure that the examination is managed properly and yields the best results possible.[86] [87]

A. How to Effectively Prepare for a Fair Lending Examination

In order to become familiar with the examination process, your bank's fair lending compliance staff should start by reviewing the relevant examination procedures from the CFPB or applicable prudential regulator, depending upon which regulator is responsible for conducting your bank's fair lending examination. Although all of the federal regulators base their exam procedures on the Interagency Fair Lending Examination Procedures created by the Federal Financial Institution Examinations Council, each regulator takes a slightly different approach. Therefore, it is important for your compliance staff to be familiar with the entire set of examination procedures for your primary fair lending regulator.

Your bank's legal department should also stay abreast of new and revised fair lending laws, regulations, and other relevant regulatory guidance. It is important to be aware of areas where the regulators have expressed concern because these are likely to be areas of focus during the examination. For example, in the CFPB's recent annual Fair Lending Report to Congress, the Bureau noted that Director Rohit Chopra has prioritized financial inclusion, racial and economic equity, and fair competition. As a result, the CFPB has focused its fair lending work on issues pertinent to people and communities of color at risk of losing their housing or unable to access credit for their small businesses. Specifically, the CFPB focused its fair lending supervision efforts on mortgage origination (underwriting, pricing and redlining), small business lending (the Section 1071 data collection and reporting rulemaking required by the Dodd-Frank Act), student loan origination, policies and procedures regarding geographic and other exclusions in underwriting, and the use of artificial intelligence (AI) and machine learning models.[88] The CFPB also noted that it will be sharpening its focus on digital redlining and algorithmic bias going forward by working to identify emerging risks and to develop appropriate policy responses.[89] In addition, the Bureau will also be analyzing how unfair and discriminatory practices harm specific population segments.[90]

Knowing your regulator's priorities can help your bank proactively assess whether its controls and fair lending program are consistent with regulatory expectations and industry best practices. Knowing these priorities can also help your bank anticipate any potential concerns that could be raised by the examiners.

Regulators use a risk-based prioritization process to determine which legal entities and/or products pose the greatest risk of lending discrimination. Factors that feed into this process may include fair lending complaints, public or private litigation, information gathered from prior fair lending examinations or enforcement actions, the adequacy and quality of your bank's fair lending program, quantitative analyses, and research or insight from the CFPB's Research, Markets, and Regulations division. Before the examination gets underway, your bank should ensure that it has appropriately addressed any issues with its fair lending program, policies, procedures, or controls that may have been cited in past examinations, audits, or risk assessments.

Even if your bank has not yet received notice of a fair lending examination, it is not too early to begin pulling and organizing documents, such as policies and procedures, which are likely to be requested by the examiners. This is because the regulators may not give your bank ample notice of a fair lending examination. In the same vein, to the extent your bank becomes aware of weaknesses that a regulator is likely to discover, legal and compliance staff should consider preparing draft narrative responses in advance.

Areas within your bank that present high fair lending risk should receive special attention. As a bank director, you should be apprised of those issues, and consider participating in intensive briefings. We have seen examination outcomes that have been undermined when bank directors could not answer basic questions by examiners or discuss issues with examiners that board minutes indicated were the subject of deliberation and action.

Furthermore, it is not too early for compliance staff to provide examination management training for employees who may interface with examiners and to identify the person who will serve as the day-to-day contact for the examiners. In addition, examiners are increasingly meeting with individual members of the board or the board as a whole to discuss examination issues. Therefore, those board members need to prepare thoroughly for such meetings.

As a bank director, it is important to know that certain information that examiners request may be protected by the attorney-client privilege. Banks should identify documents as privileged, where appropriate, when producing them to the regulators to avoid waiving the privilege with respect to third parties. Although generally most information and document requests in the examination context are not subject to typical privilege protections, to the extent that they are, the production of information or documents to the CFPB, or any regulator for that matter, does not waive any privilege that may be claimed with respect to third parties.[91]

B.   How to Effectively Manage the Fair Lending Examination Process

Even though the board of directors typically does not get involved in day-to-day management of a fair lending examination, bank directors should receive periodic updates about the examination from compliance and legal staff.

During the examination, your bank's regulatory relationship manager should be the central point of contact for the examiner in charge. In smaller institutions, that person may be a very senior officer, including the CEO. Banks should engage in a dialogue with the examiners early and often throughout the examination, especially so you can promptly respond to any potential issues or weaknesses cited by the examiners. Early notice from an examiner that a violation may have occurred will allow your bank to provide the examiner with additional information that may address the concern or demonstrate that there was no violation, clarify any misunderstanding that the examiner may have, or alert you to a previously unidentified issue that the bank can begin to investigate.

Even though your bank may have a good relationship with the examiner, it is important to treat all of the examiner's questions, no matter how informal the communication, as a formal inquiry. It is important to ensure that all requests are appropriately reviewed and considered, and that all responses are complete, accurate, and subject to review by the appropriate bank personnel, especially legal and compliance staff. When having discussions of crucial importance relating to the examination in which a written response is not required, it is still beneficial to document the conversation in writing by either sending a letter or email to the examiner, drafting an internal memorandum to file, or taking contemporaneous notes of the conversation. In addition, it is critical to monitor and track all inquiries received from the examination team and responses provided by your bank in an Excel spreadsheet or database as part of your bank's written records of the fair lending examination. The reason is because that record is often needed for future reference in managing the examination and any supervisory issues or enforcement actions that may arise as a result of the exam.

C. "Soft" Exit Meeting with Examiners

At the end of the examination, it is customary for the regulators to hold a "soft" exit meeting, where the examiners will preview their preliminary findings (which may include potential violations of law) that they intend to memorialize in the final report. Banks should use the soft exit meeting as an opportunity to discuss in depth the issues examiners have identified during the examination. It is important for your bank to recognize that these findings are not necessarily final. The final outcome could be changed, especially if the examiners' findings are based on a misunderstanding of the facts. To the extent that your bank does not agree with the examiners' preliminary findings or statement of the facts, your bank should advocate for a more accurate or favorable result by immediately clarifying any misunderstanding in writing that the examiners may have or providing in writing any additional information to justify another

69

result. And if your bank learns of intent by the examiners to refer an alleged "pattern or practice" discrimination violation to the DOJ or to recommend an enforcement action, the bank, in consultation with internal or external legal counsel, should then quickly prepare a detailed written response to the examiners' concerns before the referral or recommendation is actually made.

D.   What to Do After the Regulators Have Left

Through the process of engaging the examiner during the on-site examination and information learned during the soft exit meeting, your bank should be able to anticipate what some of the findings will be. Furthermore, to the extent you know or expect the final examination report will likely require certain changes, keep in mind that the final examination report may not give your bank very much time to implement the changes. As such, your bank will only benefit by taking advantage of the additional time and commencing corrective action and/or consumer remediation promptly.

As discussed in subsection C above, a bank may be able to change the final result of the examination if it can quickly and effectively address any deficiencies identified during the soft exit meeting. Sometimes examiners may modify the language their reports if they observe that the bank has made meaningful progress toward resolving the finding.

E.   Formal Exit Meeting

At the formal exit meeting, the regulators will typically issue their final observations in an examination report. Depending on the nature of the examiners' findings or scope of the examination, a supervisory letter may be issued instead of a full report of examination. Unlike the soft exit meeting, there is no opportunity for a bank to advocate for changes in the document because the results have been memorialized in a final report or letter.

If the board of directors and/or management team disagree with the findings of the examination report, an appeals process may be available depending on the finding that your bank wishes to dispute. It is advisable to consult your internal or external legal counsel concerning how the process works and whether your institution can avail itself of the appeals process under the circumstances presented. Banks may also avail themselves of the agency's office of the ombudsman to seek informal guidance, ask for information about the appeals process, or have the ombudsman serve as a neutral facilitator for communication between the bank and the agency. The appeals process will vary depending on your bank's prudential regulator. The OCC's Ombudsman, for instance, has authority to make binding decisions. The role of Ombudsman is somewhat different for the FRB and the FDIC. Those agencies have committees that will consider an appeal, and their Ombudsmen serve as liaisons to the agency and the bank throughout that process.

Following the issuance of the examination report, the board's role is to provide guidance to management and assistance in determining whether to pursue an appeal.

CHAPTER VIII. HMDA – GETTING IT RIGHT AND KNOWING YOUR DATA

HMDA was enacted by Congress in 1975 in response to the rising public concern that financial institutions were not meeting the mortgage loan needs of certain urban neighborhoods. HMDA and its implementing regulation, Regulation C, are designed to provide a mortgage-related data collection and reporting mechanism that allows financial institutions, regulators, and the public at large to determine whether financial institutions are failing to meet the housing needs of their communities and/or are engaging in discriminatory lending practices.

In 2011, the Dodd-Frank Act transferred rulemaking authority under HMDA from the FRB to the CFPB. The CFPB now shares enforcement authority for HMDA with the FRB, OCC, FDIC, NCUA, and HUD. As discussed in this Chapter, the agencies have placed great emphasis on accurate HMDA data and entered into public and non-public enforcement actions against banks and non-banks that have failed to provide those data.

As further discussed in this Chapter, the CFPB and prudential regulators use HMDA data as a screening mechanism for fair lending examinations to determine areas of mortgage lending risk.

A.   HMDA Compliance Requirements

1.   Data Collection, Reporting, and Public Disclosure

HMDA disclosure requirements apply to banks, savings associations and credit unions, and certain non-depository financial institutions, such as state-licensed mortgage lenders. A lender may be exempt from HMDA data collection and reporting based on its asset size, location, or volume of residential mortgage lending.

Every year, lenders that are subject to HMDA must record and disclose certain information regarding applications for, and originations and purchases of, home purchase loans and refinances.[92] Lenders must also report information on applications that did not result in originations; these include denials, incomplete applications, and applications that the lender approved but the applicant chose not to accept.[93]

Data must be collected on a loan-by-loan or application-by-application basis and compiled into a loan application register ("LAR").[94] Financial institutions must upload their LARs to the CFPB's HMDA Filing Platform and certify the accuracy and completeness of the data.[95] The Federal Financial Institutions Examination Council ("FFIEC"),[96] in turn, uses the LAR data and produces aggregate level tables incorporating geographic information by metropolitan statistical areas ("MSAs") and census tracts defined by the United States Census Bureau. The LAR data are often referred to as "HMDA data." HMDA data are intended to show lending patterns by property location, age of housing stock, income level, sex, ethnicity, and race.

The CFPB provides a web-based tool that provides consumers with online, user-friendly access to HMDA data.[97] Individuals browsing the CFPB's website can sort publicly-available HMDA data into maps and charts, which could be used to identify potential discriminatory trends or practices. This tool increases the ability of consumers and community groups to interact with HMDA data, which may give rise to discrimination complaints and/or fair lending-related litigation. In 2022, the CFPB published a *Beginner's Guide to Accessing and Using Home Mortgage Disclosure Act Data*, a resource designed to facilitate and encourage a range of stakeholders, including community groups, in accessing and using this information and to draw their own conclusions about financial institutions' HMDA data.[98]

2. Data Accuracy

As part of its supervision of larger banks and nonbank mortgage lenders, the CFPB reviews the accuracy of HMDA data and the adequacy of HMDA compliance programs. As the agency with rulemaking authority for HMDA, the CFPB has emphasized in its guidance that HMDA data integrity is vital to carrying out the purposes of the statute. Lenders required to file a LAR pursuant to HMDA and Regulation C[99] should therefore take active steps to implement an appropriate and effective compliance management system to ensure data accuracy. According to the CFPB, an effective HMDA compliance management system generally has the following attributes:

- Comprehensive policies, procedures, and internal controls to ensure ongoing HMDA and Regulation C compliance.

- Pre-submission HMDA audits that evaluate data accuracy and recommend corrective action as needed.

- Ongoing monitoring to keep the institution apprised of any regulatory changes that may have occurred since the last data collection cycle and/or supervisory examination.

- Employees who are specifically responsible for HMDA compliance, and who receive periodic and appropriate training regarding HMDA and Regulation C standards.

- Appropriate oversight by the institution's board of directors and senior management.[100]

It is the responsibility of the board of directors to provide oversight and senior management to ensure that their institution develops and maintains a HMDA compliance management system that is appropriately tailored to the size, scope, and complexity of the entity's lending operations.

Recognizing that most LARs will contain some errors, the FFIEC issued HMDA Examiner Testing Guidelines which modified previous error resubmission thresholds, established allowable tolerances for certain data fields, and established that examiners may direct financial institutions to change their compliance management systems to prevent future errors.[101]

3. Enforcement of HMDA and Regulation C

Compliance with HMDA is enforced by the CFPB, FRB, OCC, FDIC, NCUA, and HUD. Failure to record or submit accurate HMDA data can result in administrative enforcement action being taken against the financial institution, including civil money penalties.

In deciding whether or not to pursue a public enforcement action for a violation of HMDA, the CFPB considers all relevant factors, including the size of an institution's LAR and the observed error rate; whether an institution self-identified its LAR errors outside of the examination context and independently took corrective action; and, for institutions that have previously been on notice of LAR errors, whether error rates have increased or have decreased sufficiently to show substantial progress in improving HMDA compliance management.

The CFPB has repeatedly shown its willingness to use civil money penalties as an enforcement tool for HMDA violations, and since 2013, the Bureau has brought 5 HMDA enforcement actions – two of which involved significant civil money penalties.

In 2017, the CFPB entered into a consent order with Nationstar Mortgage ("Nationstar") alleging that the company's mortgage loan data contained substantial errors in violation of HMDA. Nationstar was required to pay the Bureau a civil money penalty of $1.75 million.[102] The Bureau alleged that Nationstar consistently failed to report accurate data about mortgage transactions for 2012 through 2014 despite being on notice since 2011 about its HMDA compliance problems. In addition to paying the penalty, Nationstar was required to develop and implement an effective HMDA compliance program and resubmit accurate LARs for the years at issue. The large fine stemmed from Nationstar's market share, the substantial magnitude of its errors, and its history of previous violations.

Then in 2019, the CFPB similarly required Freedom Mortgage to pay a civil money penalty of $1.75 million for submitting mortgage loan data that contained significant errors.[103] According to the consent order, the Bureau found that Freedom Mortgage violated HMDA and Regulation C by submitting mortgage loan data for 2014 to 2017 that contained significant errors. Specifically, the CFPB found that Freedom reported inaccurate race, ethnicity, and sex information and that much of Freedom's loan officers' recording of this incorrect information was intentional. For example, certain loan officers were told by managers or other loan officers that, when applicants did not provide their race or ethnicity, they should select non-Hispanic white regardless of whether that was accurate. These are the largest civil money penalties levied against HMDA reporters to date.

In 2013 and again in 2020, the CFPB entered into consent orders for $34,000 and $200,000, respectively, with Washington Federal Bank ("Washington Federal") due to its alleged failures to submit accurate HMDA data.[104] The 2020 consent order against Washington Federal required it to hire an independent consultant to review all systems, programs, policies, and procedures to ensure the accuracy of, and to prevent, identify, and correct errors in, its HMDA data. The consultant was also required to develop and implement a HMDA compliance-management system, develop and implement an audit program to regularly test HMDA data, and develop and maintain policies and procedures to ensure an understanding of HMDA standards and reporting requirements. The consent order provided that Washington Federal's comprehensive compliance plan must be provided to the CFPB for its review and that revisions requested by the Bureau must be implemented. HMDA-related consent orders regularly require the correction and resubmission of HMDA data.[105]

Given the potential costs arising from a HMDA violation and the frequent requirement to resubmit a LAR, financial institutions subject to HMDA's reporting requirements should make it a priority to develop and maintain an effective HMDA compliance management system, as described above. Although Regulation C contains a provision on bona fide errors, which provides that an error in compiling or recording HMDA data is not considered a violation if it was unintentional and occurred despite the existence and maintenance of procedures reasonably designed to prevent such errors,[106] an error rate that exceeds the permissible thresholds would most likely result in a determination that the institution's procedures were not reasonably designed to prevent such errors. It is the board of directors' role to ensure that your bank maintains a robust compliance management system with sufficient staffing and resources, as well as employee HMDA compliance training, to significantly reduce HMDA data errors, which in turn lessens the chance of a HMDA violation.

B.   Supervisory Use of HMDA Data

1.   Fair Lending Examinations

Regulators regularly use HMDA data in connection with mortgage-related fair lending and CRA examinations, so it is important for your bank to routinely run its own analysis of its HMDA data (at least annually or perhaps quarterly, depending on mortgage loan volume) to understand and defend it. Because HMDA data are not entirely comprehensive, regulators typically use the data as a screening mechanism to look for potential fair lending issues, rather than as the ultimate basis for an examination finding of discrimination or an enforcement action. By running its own HMDA analyses, banks can point to other factors involved in a particular credit decision or pricing that the HMDA data may not reflect.

Examiners, for instance, often rely upon HMDA data to determine which areas of an institution's lending operations appear to result in the disparate treatment of, or disparate impact on, protected borrowers or applicants. An examiner might run statistical analyses of an entity's HMDA data to evaluate, for example, the denial rate for minority applicants as compared with control group (white non-Hispanic) denial rates. If there is a statistically significant difference between the two denial rates, the examiner would then review and compare loan files before making an examination finding of potential discrimination.

Examiners also rely upon HMDA data to support inferences that banks may be engaging in redlining in certain metropolitan regions. In these cases, the regulator will utilize a bank's HMDA data to determine the bank's application volume in majority-minority census tracts compared to non-majority-minority census tracts. If it appears that a bank is serving predominantly minority neighborhoods significantly less than predominantly white neighborhoods, the regulators may perceive this as evidence of potential redlining.

In responding to a regulatory or an enforcement agency's claims of redlining or other discriminatory lending practices on the basis of HMDA data, lenders can point to the incomplete nature of HMDA data, which often fail to reflect the full range of a bank's lending activities. If an inquiry arises from circumstances other than an examination, preliminary analyses may be based only on data in the public LAR, which limits the reliability of any statistical results. Whether a fair lending claim is raised by a regulator or enforcement agency, institutions should develop their own competing analyses (and conduct file reviews, where appropriate) to try and demonstrate the non-discriminatory reasons for the perceived disparate treatment or disparate impact.

2.   Transactions Requiring Supervisory Approval

Regulators also consider HMDA data when approving or disapproving applications submitted by banks seeking to engage in certain transactions, including establishing new branches or merging with or acquiring another institution, as described below.

a.   Branching

When determining whether or not to approve a bank's application to establish additional branch offices, regulators often consider the bank's compliance with the fair lending laws. This may include an analysis of HMDA data, particularly if public comments have been submitted in response to the application that include arguments based upon HMDA data. However, the regulators acknowledge that critical data regarding a bank's lending decisions are not fully reported under HMDA, and may seek to supplement their analysis accordingly with a bank's internal analysis reflecting additional lending data and/or non-HMDA-based reasoning.

In order to facilitate a regulatory decision regarding a branching application, a bank should be prepared to provide the regulators with additional statistical analyses and reports based upon additional data and other proprietary information pertaining to its lending operations. This additional information may refute or explain any problematic HMDA statistics relied upon by the agency.

b.   Mergers and Acquisitions

Regulators also consider HMDA data when making a determination regarding an application to combine two institutions or where one financial institution seeks to acquire another. As with applications for additional branches, regulators may directly address HMDA data in their analysis, especially in response to public comments based upon HMDA statistics. Applicant banks seeking approval to merge or acquire another financial institution should be able to provide the regulators with their own statistical analyses and reports based upon non-HMDA data to demonstrate compliance with fair lending and CRA requirements. When one bank in a proposed merger has been cited with a fair lending violation, the regulator typically focuses on whether the other bank in the proposed merger has a robust fair lending compliance program that is equipped to address any potential deficiencies at the other institution. When both banks involved in a proposed merger are addressing fair lending violations or investigations, this factor generally serves as an impediment to approval of the merger until one or both issues are resolved.

C.   Public Use of HMDA Data

1.   Private Litigation

Private litigants — individuals and groups — also rely on publicly available HMDA data in pursuing discrimination claims against lenders.[107] In the past, class action suits have been filed against mortgage lenders based upon HMDA statistical analyses that appeared to suggest that minority mortgage applicants were treated less favorably than white applicants.

For example, in *Ramirez v. GreenPoint Mortgage Funding, Inc.,*[108] three minority borrowers who obtained mortgage loans from GreenPoint Mortgage Funding ("GreenPoint") brought a class action alleging that GreenPoint violated the FHA and the ECOA by charging minority borrowers disproportionately high rates compared to non-minority borrowers with the same credit risk profile. The plaintiffs successfully made a *prima facie* case that alleged pricing discrimination occurred on the basis of statistical analyses of HMDA data,[109] and GreenPoint subsequently settled for $14.75 million.

The fact that public HMDA data alone cannot be used to comprehensively analyze a bank's lending practices, however, proves to be a significant challenge for private litigants whose primary source of empirical evidence is HMDA data.

Banks frequently defend against HMDA-based claims by questioning the validity of any conclusions drawn by the plaintiff without critical information regarding the borrower and collateral. However, challenging the validity of a complainant's statistical results is generally effective only if the lender can propose a more robust data set or model that disproves a statistically significant disparity.

2.   Community Group Action

Since the 1990s, community groups have used HMDA data to investigate, publicize, and combat perceived discriminatory lending patterns, particularly in urban areas with a significant minority population.[110] Community groups have relied upon a variety of approaches to accomplish their goals, including protests to applications for mergers or acquisitions, administrative complaints, public awareness campaigns, complaints to financial regulators and enforcement agencies, and private agreements with financial institutions. While community groups frequently rely on the statistical analysis of publicly available HMDA data to support their fair lending claims, they sometimes support such claims by conducting "mystery shopping."

Example: St. Louis Metropolitan Area

The St. Louis, Missouri metropolitan area has long been the focus of community group pressure based on HMDA data. Since the Association of Community Organizations for Reform Now ("ACORN") launched its first anti-redlining campaign in St. Louis in 1976, lenders in the St. Louis area have found themselves the subjects of ongoing fair lending scrutiny based upon their HMDA data. Even after decades of negotiations and agreements between local community groups and St. Louis-area mortgage lenders, claims of redlining and other fair lending concerns persist.

A settlement between the Metropolitan St. Louis Equal Housing Opportunity Council ("Metropolitan St. Louis EHOC") and First National Bank of St. Louis ("FNBSL") indicates that community groups in St. Louis remain active in their pursuit of fair lending reform at local financial institutions. This agreement, which was approved by HUD in 2010, resolved a complaint filed by Metropolitan St. Louis EHOC alleging that FNBSL excluded areas with a high concentration of minorities in its lending operations and branch office offerings.[111] As part of the settlement, FNBSL was required to implement a variety of outreach, educational, and special financing initiatives directed toward minority communities in the St. Louis metropolitan region.

The St. Louis metropolitan area example serves as a reminder to the leadership of financial institutions, particularly those in urban areas, that community groups remain powerful advocacy forces in the area of fair lending. The board and senior management of financial institutions located in geographic areas with a strong community group presence should be open to dialogue with these groups outside of the regulatory context.

Privately-negotiated partnerships with community groups can serve to improve access to credit for minorities, enhance an institution's local reputation, reduce fair lending risk, and avoid administrative intervention and/or costly litigation expenses.

D.   The Future of HMDA Data and Its Use

As technology reduces the burdens of accessing and analyzing HMDA data and with the CFPB actively encouraging individuals and community groups leverage it for their own purposes, lenders should expect that fair lending regulatory and litigation challenges based upon HMDA information will continue in the future.

In November 2021, the CFPB issued a Request for Information to the public, seeking input on rules implementing HMDA. The stated purpose of this request was to evaluate the effectiveness of HMDA's rules and to strengthen the CFPB's ability to maintain a fair, competitive, and non-discriminatory mortgage market. The comment period closed in 2022. It is unclear at this time how or when the CFPB will use the comments and feedback it collected. Nonetheless, it is clear that the Bureau will continue to focus on HMDA data integrity and continue to use the data to bring enforcement actions going forward.

CHAPTER IX. AN INTRODUCTION TO FAIR LENDING STATISTICAL ANALYSES – MAKING SENSE OF YOUR BANK'S DATA

In recent years, fair lending monitoring and testing has become a regulatory expectation for banks of all sizes. Likewise, regulators, private plaintiffs, and consumer advocacy groups are using statistical evidence to support their discrimination claims for both mortgage and non-mortgage products. Regulators also rely on statistical analyses prior to examinations in order to determine a focal point for the examination and during the examination to identify potential fair lending violations. The CFPB in particular has publicly stated that it is using a "data-driven" approach to shape its supervisory and enforcement priorities at both the bank and market levels.[112]

As a bank director, you are not responsible for managing the day-to-day aspects of your bank's fair lending analytical program. However, you are expected to understand your bank's fair lending risk profile and what controls are in place to identify and address those risks. To effectively execute those responsibilities, it is useful for you to have a basic understanding of how statistical methods are used to assess and enforce compliance with fair lending laws and regulations. The purpose of this Chapter is to provide you with that understanding.

A. Why Your Bank Should Consider Conducting Fair Lending Statistical Analyses

Today, many banks incorporate monitoring and testing into their fair lending compliance programs to better understand their fair lending risks and how the data could be used by regulators, private plaintiffs, and consumer advocates to allege potential violations of the fair lending laws. As discussed in Chapters III and IV, fair lending risk may be associated with your bank's products, lending channels, lending and servicing practices, and marketing efforts.

Using statistical analyses, your bank can get a preview of how a regulator or litigation adversary will look for violations of fair lending laws, and use that information to develop a risk-based approach to ensure that priority is given to areas within the bank that present the highest quantitative fair lending risk. In Chapter VI, we discussed the importance of establishing policies, procedures, and other controls to mitigate fair lending risk across your bank's credit business. Statistical analyses can be used, in part, to test the effectiveness of those controls.

In addition, banks that take a deeper dive into their data may successfully rebut allegations of discrimination by finding flaws in the claimant's statistical analysis and presenting an alternative analysis that shows that the policy or practice at issue was not discriminatory. This task is much easier if the bank has already conducted its own statistical analysis; starting from scratch under the time pressure of an allegation of discrimination is much more difficult.

It is important to recognize that there is no "one size fits all" formula for developing a bank's fair lending statistical analysis program. Ultimately, the analyses that your bank performs (and the frequency in which they are performed) will depend on myriad factors, including your bank's size, complexity, product mix, underwriting methods (judgmental vs. automated), loan volume, risk appetite, and resources.

B.   Collection and Use of Data for Fair Lending Statistical Analyses

Fair lending professionals frequently quote the old adage "garbage in, garbage out," which means that imperfect data will lead to unreliable results. There are several reasons why compilation of data for fair lending analysis is challenging, especially for banks that have not engaged in the process before.

First, data is not always available or easily accessible. For instance, it may be difficult or impossible to account for critical factors in a statistical analysis because those factors are qualitative in nature (*e.g.,* conversations with underwriters which are memorialized in loan files) or because the data simply may not exist (*e.g.*, race, ethnicity, and sex cannot be collected by law for non-mortgage credit products).

Second, data integrity may also present obstacles to an accurate statistical result, particularly where multiple systems have conflicting data. For instance, the reliability and completeness of the available data may be compromised due to human data entry errors, or by information being overwritten during the consideration of an application. So, while statistical analyses can provide helpful insight into a bank's fair lending risk, those results are only as good as the underlying data. One of the benefits of performing a statistical analysis as a compliance measure is that it gives the bank the opportunity to discover and correct these kinds of data quality issues, when the bank is not under time pressure to produce information to a regulator or defend itself against a claim of discrimination.

In general, there are two sources of prohibited basis group data that are used to conduct fair lending statistical analyses: (1) HMDA data for mortgage loans, and (2) proxy methods for non-mortgage loans.

1.   Using HMDA Data

In accordance with Regulation B, mortgage lenders must ask (but may not require) applicants to identify their ethnicity, race, sex, and marital status when applying for a loan secured by a dwelling that is occupied (or will be occupied) by the applicant.[113] Borrower demographic data that is compiled and reported pursuant to HMDA and Regulation C include only race, ethnicity, and sex for the applicant and co-applicant.[114] HMDA data are used by regulators, consumer advocacy groups, and private plaintiffs to "assist in identifying possible discriminatory lending patterns and enforcing antidiscrimination statutes."[115]

Using HMDA data, a regulator could develop a statistical model to identify potential differences in mortgage loan pricing for minority borrowers and non-Hispanic white borrowers. Although today's HMDA data do not incorporate all of the non-discriminatory and objective factors used by a bank to evaluate any given loan application, such as the applicant's credit score, the applicant's debt-to-income ratio, or the loan-to-value ratio, a regulator will have access to that information from the bank's loan origination system or underwriting data, and it can be combined with the protected class information collected via HMDA to enable an analysis of whether members of protected classes experienced different outcomes in underwriting or pricing, even when credit-related factors are controlled for. A bank's internal statistical analysis would use the same methodology.

2. Using Proxy Methods

Fair lending statistical analysis for non-mortgage credit products carries an additional hurdle, because fair lending laws and regulations prohibit lenders from collecting data on race, ethnicity, sex, and other prohibited basis characteristics for these applicants.[116] In the absence of data identifying applicants' or borrowers' protected class status, regulators use proxies to estimate the ethnicity, race, sex, and other protected group characteristics for non-mortgage loan applicants. Banks' own statistical analyses typically use the same proxy method as that used by the regulatory agencies.

For example, regulators use a proxy methodology that predicts the likelihood of an applicant being Hispanic or Asian based on his or her surname. Because surname proxies are poor predictors of race, regulators typically use census tract data to predict the likelihood of an applicant being African American. An applicant's sex is typically predicted by use of first name proxies.

Beginning with a series of indirect auto enforcement actions in 2013,[117] and continuing to the present, the CFPB and the DOJ have used a proxy methodology that stems from the health care industry called Bayesian Improved Surname Geocoding ("BISG") that estimates probabilities of race and ethnicity of a borrower applicant based on a combination of the applicant's home address and surname.[118] In September 2014, the CFPB issued a "white paper" to provide more detail on its BISG proxy methodology.[119]

Even though the use of proxies can be a helpful monitoring tool, there is ample evidence that proxy methodologies frequently fail to accurately predict an applicant's or borrower's characteristics. To the contrary, an article on the predictive strength of the BISG methodology concluded that there was only a 76% correlation between the assigned BISG proxy and the self-reported race or ethnicity of the subjects.[120]

Similarly, a 2014 study conducted by Charles River Associates that was commissioned by the American Financial Services Association ("AFSA") regarding indirect auto retail installment sales contracts found that the BISG proxy methodology resulted in significant bias and high error rates.[121] AFSA's study calculated BISG probabilities against a test population of HMDA data, where actual race and ethnicity are known. Those results revealed that BISG failed to identify three out of four African American applicants and four out of 10 Hispanic applicants.[122] The AFSA study concluded that while the BISG proxy methodology "may be relatively less inaccurate than geography-only and name-only proxy methods, the methodology is characterized by objectively high error rates."[123]

Nevertheless, regulators have embraced the use of BISG as authoritative, and routinely use it for fair lending analyses of non-mortgage credit products. For that reason, banks performing their own internal statistical testing should do the same.

C. Using Statistical Analyses to Assess Your Bank's Fair Lending Performance

1. Understanding the Types of Fair Lending Reviews

There are two common tools used in fair lending statistical reviews that can help a lender identify potential fair lending risk: regression analysis and file reviews. These reviews can help a lender identify differences in credit decision or pricing outcomes and the factors that may be driving those differences.

Regression analysis is a statistical analysis of application data for a particular lending channel (*e.g.*, mortgage, credit card, auto) that is usually further segmented by loan product (*e.g.*, prime vs. nonprime or conforming vs. non-conforming).

Unlike a "raw" statistical analysis that only looks for disparities without any explanatory variables, a regression model will take into account important explanatory variables that may have impacted the pricing or underwriting decision, including credit score, property type, debt-to-income ratio, loan-to-value ratio, and prior bankruptcies or foreclosures. By analyzing the data with a regression model, lenders are evaluating applicants in an "apples-to-apples" approach, to see if similarly situated applicants received different outcomes that seem to be explained only by protected characteristics under the fair lending laws.

Historically, fair lending regression analyses alone have not been considered sufficient evidence to establish a discrimination claim by a regulator or enforcement agency. However, the CFPB has recently been pursuing fair lending investigations or supervisory actions against lenders where the results of a regression analysis alone have formed the basis of an allegation. Where the results of a regression analysis show that there is a statistically significant disparity in pricing or underwriting that is adverse to a prohibited basis group, lenders commonly elect to review loan files for three reasons. First, the files may reveal that certain data fields were excluded from the regression model that have a material impact on the statistical results, allowing the bank to update the regression analysis to include the missing data. Second, the files may show legitimate non-discriminatory reasons for the decisions that are not captured in the loan data (*e.g.*, ineligible collateral, failure to provide the necessary documentation to complete the application process, appraisal value did not support the requested loan amount, etc.). Third, the file review may identify that there is a data integrity issue (*e.g.*, the decline reason in the data does not reflect the decline reason in the loan file).

Where outliers are identified in a regression analysis, a file review can be a helpful tool in determining whether the loan files reveal legitimate and non-discriminatory reasons to explain the differential treatment of applicants or borrowers that cannot be captured in the data used for regression analysis. As noted above, a file review may reveal potential data integrity issues or data points that were omitted from the regression model that may be an appropriate variable to include.

File reviews typically involve a review of any hard copy or electronic loan files, including notes and emails, as well as the data and information stored in the loan origination system. The objective of such reviews is to determine whether there are non-discriminatory reasons to explain the differences observed in the statistical analysis. It is possible that some of these differences could not have been factored into a quantitative model.

File reviewers may also need to conduct interviews of loan originators or underwriters for added context, particularly where the documentation in the file is sparse. In some cases, a bank may need to consult with a third party engaged in the origination process, such as a mortgage broker or auto lender, for information about the credit decision or pricing outcome. Ideally, supplemental interviews would not be necessary because the loan files should be well-documented and provide enough detail to explain credit decisions or pricing outcomes, but such documentation is often limited. Because poorly-documented application decisions can themselves increase a bank's fair lending risk, a file review can also suggest documentation practices as an area of improvement for the bank's operations.

It is important to train file reviewers about the requisite information to collect during the file review and how that information should be captured in the results. If analysis is required by the file reviewer, the file reviewer should not be asked to determine whether there is evidence of discrimination, which is only appropriate for legal counsel. The file reviewer should only be determining whether there is evidence in the file to support the pricing or underwriting decision.

a.   Comparative File Reviews

In some instances, a bank may elect only to review "outlier files," which, in the context of underwriting, are the prohibited basis group applications that the regression model predicted to be approved but were declined, and the control group applications that the model predicted to be declined but were approved. For pricing, outlier files may be reviewed for prohibited basis group applicants where the regression model predicted pricing that is less than the actual price given to the protected basis group applicant and the predicted pricing for control group applicants is more than the pricing actually provided to the control group applicant.

Regulators tend to prefer comparative file reviews, which look at a sample of outlier files from a prohibited basis group and similarly situated control group borrowers to serve as comparators. The objective is to determine whether similarly situated applicants received similar treatment during the pricing or underwriting process.

As an initial step, the bank must choose the appropriate focal points for the review. The most meaningful comparative file reviews focus on a specific loan product, time frame, geographic region, or phase of the credit administration process.

Next, the bank should identify the appropriate sample of loans, which is usually accomplished by focusing on marginal applicants or borrowers. Marginal applicants consist of approved and denied applications that were not clearly qualified or unqualified based on the bank's underwriting criteria.

These include, among other things, applications that a more conservative loan officer might have denied, applications that narrowly met or failed the bank's written guidelines, and applications for which certain creditworthiness requirements may have been waived. FFIEC has published guidance on suggested sample sizes for comparative file reviews, which the CFPB has subsequently incorporated into its examination procedures.[124]

The file review itself compares files of individuals who belong to a protected class group (*e.g.*, women, racial or ethnic minorities) to files of individuals who are not members of a protected class. When identifying the focal points for the review, the bank should limit each review to the comparison of one protected class group. To illustrate, one review should compare the treatment of males to females, rather than compare the treatment of non-Hispanic white males to Hispanic females.

When conducting the review, a best practice is to document the reviewer's findings in a spreadsheet. With respect to each applicant or borrower, the spreadsheet should set forth the data points that are used in the credit decision or pricing process (*e.g.*, FICO, trade history, date of action, loan amount, loan-to-value ratio ("LTV"), debt-to-income ratio, etc.) as well as notes contained in the file that could justify the final outcome (*e.g.*, policy exceptions or compensating factors).

2. Using Statistical Analyses Across Your Bank's Credit Administration Process

a. Underwriting Analyses

Statistical analyses of your bank's underwriting data can help answer the question of whether applicants were subject to less favorable underwriting standards or practices because of their race, color, national origin, marital status, or some other prohibited basis. There are several types of underwriting analyses that a bank could perform.

"Accept or deny" analyses could be performed to determine whether a bank denied applications from potentially qualified protected class members but approved those from similarly situated non-protected class members. A regression model would take into account the effect of objective factors that would likely influence the underwriting outcome.

Objective factors include the characteristics of the loan (*e.g.*, LTV ratio, loan type, and requested term), characteristics of the property for mortgage loans (*e.g.*, single-family primary residence, vacation condominium, or cooperative apartment),

93

and characteristics of the applicant (*e.g.*, creditworthiness and income).

For areas of a bank's underwriting process that afford employee discretion, such as underwriting exceptions, statistical analyses could be performed to see whether applicants of a particular demographic are more likely to receive concessions than other applicants. In general, exception and override processes are areas in which regulators focus heavily in fair lending analysis because of the possibility that those exceptions of overrides may not be applied in an even-handed manner across protected class groups.

"Assistance" analyses could also be performed to assess whether similarly situated applicants received different treatment in the underwriting process. A fair lending assistance case could allege that a lender made special efforts to qualify and approve non-Hispanic white mortgage applicants but did not make the same efforts for African American and Hispanic applicants.

b.   Pricing Analyses

Statistical analyses of your bank's pricing data can help answer the question of whether borrowers received less favorable pricing terms (*e.g.*, interest rate, broker fees, origination fees, or other charges) because of their race, color, national origin, marital status, or some other prohibited basis.

There are a number of legitimate and non-discriminatory factors that could influence the ultimate pricing of a loan: credit score, loan term, loan amount, LTV ratio, and geographic variables (*e.g.*, loans sorted by state). These factors should be considered in the regression model, to the extent there is data.

It is a best practice to include a timing component in the regression model (*i.e.*, interest rate lock date or loan origination date) to account for fluctuations in interest rates and market conditions. For analyses of auto loans, a regression analysis should also distinguish between new and used vehicles, and include the model year of the collateral.

c. Redlining Analyses

Redlining cases assert that a mortgage lender has served mostly minority geographic areas (referred to as "majority-minority") less favorably than majority-white areas. A majority-minority area is an area in which more than 50 percent of the residents identify their race or ethnicity as other than non-Hispanic white.

A bank can perform redlining analyses by focusing on a single city or the larger MSA that includes a city's surrounding suburbs, and then examine the populations at the census tract level. A lender's self-delineated CRA assessment area can also serve as the appropriate area for a redlining review. The basic components of a redlining review include a "peer analysis" to see if the bank had significantly fewer applications and originated loans in majority-minority areas, and a geographic analysis that overlays the bank's CRA assessment area, branch locations, and the locations of applications and originated loans to see if there is a pattern of the bank avoiding majority-minority areas.

d. Reverse Redlining Analyses

Reverse redlining claims arise when banks steer minority borrowers to different programs within a loan type (*e.g.*, prime versus non-prime auto loans) with less favorable terms, conditions, or pricing to otherwise qualified borrowers on a prohibited basis.

A bank may conduct analyses to assess whether it made a higher proportion of nonprime loans in majority-minority areas because of nondiscriminatory, legitimate considerations. Reverse redlining analyses may consider lending activity at both the community and borrower levels. As a result, some of the analyses in reverse redlining reviews will resemble the analyses conducted in underwriting and pricing cases.

e.   Servicing Analyses

Because fair servicing is a relatively new concept, regulatory expectations and best practices in monitoring fair servicing compliance continue to evolve. It is worth noting that there are a number of impediments to the statistical analysis of loan servicing (*e.g.*, data limitations, borrower incentives, action or inaction, and investor and contractual limitations) that complicate analyses of fair servicing performance.

A bank may conduct testing and monitoring to identify statistically significant unexplained disparate loan servicing and loss mitigation outcomes between borrower groups. A bank can select similarly situated borrowers and compare levels of assistance, default servicing outcome, and modification terms. Analysis of outcomes should include the range of workout possibilities and examine the frequency, the terms, and the speed of outcomes.

A bank should also examine data related to borrowers' loss mitigation behaviors (*e.g.*, whether a borrower completes a loss mitigation package, responds to follow-up inquiries by the servicer, or accepts and abides by the terms of a proposed loss mitigation program).

3.   What Should Be Done With the Results of Your Bank's Statistical Analyses?

There are several options that your bank should consider if the results of the statistical analyses — after completion of any supplemental file reviews and investigation — suggest that disparate impact or disparate treatment may exist. For example, your bank may determine that corrective action or changes to the bank's policies and practices are warranted.

Legal or compliance personnel may issue warnings to loan officers, branches, or brokers with disparities in their lending practices and place these parties on a "watch list" until these disparities have been removed. Further, it may be determined that enhancements should be made to the bank's policies or procedures to ensure the consistent and objective treatment of applicants and borrowers in lending and servicing decisions.

With respect to specific borrowers, upon further review, the bank may decide that corrective action or remediation is necessary. The CFPB has encouraged banks to fully remediate customers affected by compliance issues in addition to taking action to correct the underlying deficiencies that gave rise to the remediation.[125] To that end, we are aware of banks that have proactively compensated borrowers based on the results of statistical analyses evidencing disparate pricing of loans. We recommend working with legal counsel to discuss potential options for carrying out the remediation of borrowers.

D.   Who Should Perform Your Bank's Statistical Analyses?

There are several factors that your bank should consider when deciding whether to conduct statistical analyses in-house or to outsource the process. If your bank conducts statistical analyses in-house, you should consider the expertise of your personnel, cost of purchasing software, and the bank's total number of applicant and borrower files. Even though there are many software packages that can help a bank perform statistical analyses, your bank should have an in-house expert in statistics, who can assist representatives in legal and compliance in interpreting the results from the analyses.

If you engage a third-party consultant to conduct your bank's statistical analyses, you should consider whether you will be able to explain the results of these analyses to your regulator and whether you could reuse the model developed. While there are certainly advantages and disadvantages to each approach, some banks use a hybrid model in which fair lending statistical analyses are initially performed by a third-party consultant and then later brought in-house. The transition of the function to the bank generally occurs after appropriate staff have been hired or trained to conduct and interpret the analyses.

Regardless of whether your bank chooses to perform your analyses in-house or to outsource the process, it is an industry best practice to perform fair lending statistical analyses at the direction and under the supervision of legal counsel. Outside counsel with expertise in fair lending are well-positioned to provide insight on emerging enforcement trends, as well as evolving regulatory expectations, and industry best practices for fair lending monitoring programs. The use of outside counsel when conducting fair lending statistical analyses also provides greater protection in establishing and maintaining attorney-client privilege.

Although the CFPB and prudential regulators do not believe that the attorney-client privilege applies to statistical analyses in a supervisory or examination context, it is still advisable to conduct such analyses under attorney-client privilege to protect them from disclosure in enforcement and litigation matters.

CHAPTER X.   WHAT TO DO IF YOUR BANK BECOMES THE TARGET OF A FAIR LENDING INVESTIGATION OR ENFORCEMENT ACTION

Fair lending investigations and enforcement actions can be lengthy, costly, and resource-intensive events for a bank. Where a regulator determines that the bank has violated a fair lending law, the matter may also result in significant reputational harm and multi-million-dollar settlements. In the event of a threatened fair lending investigation or enforcement action, it is crucial that your bank respond quickly yet strategically.

A.   How Fair Lending Investigations and Enforcement Actions Arise — and What to Expect

Typically, a fair lending investigation or enforcement action arises through the supervision and examination process. A prudential regulator (the OCC, FDIC, or FRB) or the CFPB may discover an issue during an examination that it deems to be a violation of the federal fair lending laws; occasionally, a complaint from a consumer or a whistleblower employee can also give rise to an investigation. If the alleged violation of the federal fair lending laws is an isolated incident or is not deemed to be severe, it may simply be noted in a supervisory letter or indicated as a "Matter Requiring Attention" in an examination report. If the alleged violation is deemed severe and/or constitutes a pattern or practice of alleged discrimination, then it may lead to a preliminary supervisory determination and the issuance of a "15-day letter" by the prudential regulators or a Potential Action and Request for Response ("PARR") letter by the CFPB. A 15-day letter or PARR letter is typically issued by the Washington headquarters office of the prudential regulator or CFPB.

Banks often discover the intent of an agency to pursue an enforcement action or a referral to the DOJ even before a 15-day letter or PARR letter is received through discussions with examiners while they are still on-site, at the "soft" exit meeting or formal exit meeting. Bank management and the board of directors should make every effort to address and resolve any significant fair lending issues raised either during the exam or at the soft exit meeting before the examiners finalize any conclusions. If that approach fails, bank management should remain in communication with the examination team and attempt to resolve the issue before the official exit meeting or before the bank receives a 15-day letter or PARR letter. It is often helpful to enlist the assistance of the regulator's regional office staff to attempt to resolve the matter before a 15-day or PARR letter is issued because the regional office can help staff in the Washington office better understand the facts and the bank's position on the matter. By facilitating communication, the regional office can serve as a liaison between the bank and regulators in Washington, who are the ultimate decision makers on the matter.

Both the 15-day letter and PARR letter may provide the bank with notice of preliminary findings of a violation or violations of the federal fair lending laws. If there is a potential violation that could be referred to the DOJ, then the 15-day letter or PARR letter provides the bank with notice of the potential for such a referral. The 15-day and PARR letters may also notify the bank that the regulator is considering taking supervisory action, such as a non-public memorandum of understanding, or a public enforcement action, based on potential violations identified and described in the letter.

The bank is required to respond to the 15-day letter within that prescribed timeframe and, for the CFPB's PARR letter, within 14 days, although short extensions of time can often be negotiated with the regulator. The response must set forth any reasons of fact, law, or policy concerning why the regulator should not take action against the bank and provide supporting documentation, if appropriate. In some cases, the regulator will request additional documentation after reviewing the bank's response. The information provided by the bank is designed to help the regulator determine whether it is appropriate to take supervisory or enforcement action against the bank.

If your bank receives an unfavorable supervisory letter or fair lending examination report, it might foreshadow a forthcoming investigation or enforcement action and provide time for the bank to prepare accordingly. Alternatively, a regulator may issue a civil investigative demand ("CID"), which is designed to compel production of documents, responses to interrogatories, and/or testimony of witnesses prior to instituting any legal proceedings. A CID is often unanticipated and may be prompted by consumer complaints, advocacy groups, or whistleblowers; referrals from cooperating agencies; or other factors that fuel a regulator's sense that the bank may have engaged in discriminatory practices.

If your bank first receives a CID, signaling the beginning of a regulatory investigation, it must act urgently. Under CFPB rules, for example, the bank must first "meet and confer" with investigators (to negotiate the CID's scope and the investigative process) within 10 days of receipt of the CID;[126] file any petition to amend or quash the CID within 20 days;[127] and begin to produce the often-substantial amount of requested documents, testimony, responses to written questions, or other materials within the short amount of allotted time (generally 30 days).

B.   Choosing the Right Defense Team

In light of these accelerated regulatory timelines, your bank must promptly determine the purpose and scope of the investigation and establish an appropriate response team to coordinate its defense. A lean fair lending response team might consist of the bank's general counsel, chief compliance (or fair lending) officer, chief information officer, relevant business executives, and potentially a third-party statistical consultant. Other executives or employees may be added to the team as needed.

One of the first decisions your bank needs to make in response to a fair lending inquiry or investigation is whether to retain outside counsel or to respond to the issue through internal resources. This choice is an important one because experienced fair lending counsel will be familiar with the life cycle of a fair lending enforcement investigation and can provide guidance to the bank about what to expect. They may be able to facilitate a resolution through the supervisory process rather than the enforcement process or persuade the agency that no further action is necessary.

Fair lending outside counsel can also play a critical role in negotiations that the bank would prefer not to engage in itself insofar as the dialogue creates tension in the regulatory relationship between the bank and the agency. Outside counsel may also have working relationships with the regulators and enforcement agencies that will further your bank's credibility and help you navigate the process more effectively.

On the other hand, a bank may consider handling a fair lending matter in-house if it has experienced legal counsel with the subject matter expertise, skill set, and time to handle an investigation, which may involve extensive negotiations, interrogatory responses, data submissions, investigative hearings, and meetings with the regulators. Apart from the cost savings of using in-house counsel in a fair lending matter, certain efficiencies can be gained from their preexisting institutional knowledge of the bank's operations and supervisory history. Some banks prefer to use in-house legal counsel to retain greater control over the tone of the dialogue to ensure that discussions do not become overly adversarial or to avoid the appearance that they are "lawyering up."

Each bank must factor in the costs and benefits of using in-house versus outside counsel to handle a fair lending matter, recognizing that all the risks of a seemingly innocuous inquiry are not always evident from the outset and only become apparent after some period of time.

C.   Your Board Must Stay Apprised of the Proceedings

As with fair lending examinations, the board of directors typically is not involved in the day-to-day management of a significant fair lending compliance issue arising during an examination, a fair lending investigation, or an enforcement action. Bank directors, however, must understand the nature of the investigation and oversee the bank's enforcement defense, providing consultation when necessary.

The board (or a delegated committee) should always be made aware of any informal investigative request or threatened enforcement action, and it should request periodic updates from legal counsel on the status of the investigation. Many boards appoint at least one director to serve as a liaison between the board and the response team during an open investigation to ensure regular communication between management and the board and clear direction from the board on material decisions relating to the investigation.

D.   What Is the Right Defense Strategy?

While legal counsel will advise your bank on recommended defense strategies as they become relevant, your bank and board should consider certain key issues in advance:

- *How cooperative will your bank be?* Cooperating with a regulator might foster a relationship of trust and credibility that pays off during current negotiations and future proceedings. However, being overly conciliatory can result in an adverse outcome for the bank that might have otherwise been avoided with an appropriate level of advocacy and dialogue. Refusal to cooperate is generally ill-advised insofar as it may foment distrust that results in a more aggressive investigation or enforcement action.

- *Will your bank make public a non-public proceeding?* While investigations are generally confidential, certain laws, particularly for publicly traded companies, may mandate public disclosure of enforcement proceedings. Likewise, if the bank petitions the CFPB to quash a CID, the investigation generally becomes public.[128] To the extent that public disclosure is discretionary, consider the resulting reputational harm (including anticipated media coverage, potential public relations efficacy, and employee morale) and the potential instigation of "copycat" litigation by private parties.

- *Should your bank prepare a response to a preliminary determination of a fair lending violation?* Toward the end of a fair lending examination or investigation, the regulator will notify the bank that it has made a preliminary determination of a fair lending violation and provide the bank with an opportunity to respond to the agency with additional facts or analysis that may alter their conclusion.[129] While banks may choose not to respond to an agency's letter indicating its preliminary determination of a violation, it is rarely in the bank's best interest to provide no response at all. To properly take advantage of this opportunity, many banks prepare a full legal and statistical analysis and, where appropriate, file review results.

Ultimately, the best overarching strategy is for your bank to be strategic in its management of the investigation or examination and all related communications. Your response team knows and has better access to your bank's information and data than regulators, who must continuously adapt to the facts they gather and analyses they develop throughout their investigation. The key is to think ahead and prepare to adapt your strategy to the facts and analysis as they develop.

E.   Opportunity to Mitigate Risk

Your bank should treat a fair lending inquiry or investigation as an opportunity to mitigate future fair lending risk. For example, the bank should consider whether the risks identified in the prior matter flagged the need to reform bank policies or procedures or to conduct a fair lending risk assessment of relevant business units.

Alternatively, if employees are implicated as wrongdoers in an overt discrimination or disparate treatment matter, your bank should consider appropriate disciplinary and oversight actions that will prevent reoccurrence, such as training or employee communications.

In addition, the board of directors should consider whether the prior fair lending matter identified areas where the board should expand its oversight of fair lending compliance, as discussed in Chapter II.

APPENDIX A: FAIR LENDING LAWS & REGULATIONS

This Appendix A provides a brief overview of two primary federal fair lending laws, the ECOA and the FHAct. Both the ECOA and the FHAct prohibit discrimination on specific bases. Some state and local fair lending laws may contain additional prohibited bases that are not discussed in this Handbook. This Appendix A also provides a brief overview of key federal laws that are related to fair lending, but are not fair lending laws *per se*.

A.   Equal Credit Opportunity Act

The ECOA, which is implemented by Regulation B, is primarily enforced by the CFPB. The ECOA was enacted in 1974 following hearings held by the National Commission on Consumer Finance in 1972, which demonstrated that women faced significant difficulties in attempting to obtain access to consumer credit. As a result, the focus of the original version of the ECOA was on women, with the stated purpose of the law being to require financial institutions engaged in extending credit to make credit "equally available to all creditworthy customers *without regard to sex or marital status*."[130] Subsequent amendments to the ECOA in 1976 added seven additional prohibited bases to broaden the law's antidiscrimination requirements.[131]

The ECOA makes it unlawful for any creditor to discriminate against an applicant on a prohibited basis during any aspect of a credit transaction.[132] The ECOA also makes it unlawful for any creditor to discourage a reasonable person from making or pursuing an application on a prohibited basis. The prohibited bases under the ECOA are:

ECOA Prohibited Bases
<ul><li>Race</li><li>National origin</li><li>Color</li><li>Religion</li><li>Sex (including sexual orientation and gender identity)</li><li>Age</li><li>Receipt of public assistance income</li><li>Marital status</li><li>A consumer's good faith exercise of any right under the Consumer Credit Protection Act</li></ul>

The ECOA applies to both consumer and commercial credit, including both mortgage and non-mortgage lending products. The ECOA applies to the entire credit life cycle, from new product development, marketing and advertising through servicing, collections, and foreclosure or repossession.

Regulation B imposes additional technical requirements that are intended to further the purpose of the ECOA, including particular actions within the lending and servicing process that are prohibited, permitted, or required. Regulation B contains an Official Staff Commentary ("Commentary") that was originally issued by the FRB and subsequently adopted by the CFPB, which further interprets the ECOA's requirements.[133] It is a good practice for your bank's legal and compliance staff to review the Commentary to further understand the requirements of Regulation B.

1.   Supervisory and Enforcement Authority over the ECOA

Numerous federal agencies share supervision and enforcement authority for the ECOA.[134] The CFPB has authority to promulgate rules under the ECOA. The CFPB also has primary supervisory and enforcement authority for the ECOA over banks and non-banks with more than $10 billion in assets that offer consumer loan products or services or engage in consumer lending. The prudential regulators — the FRB, OCC, and the FDIC — have supervisory and enforcement authority for the ECOA for banks with less than $10 billion in assets. The FTC has overlapping supervisory and enforcement authority for the ECOA with the CFPB over non-banks that offer consumer loan products or services.[135] The DOJ conducts investigations of "pattern or practice" The ECOA violations referred to it by the CFPB and prudential regulators, and it may also initiate its own investigations.

The ECOA also provides for private rights of action, whereby individual plaintiffs may seek civil damages in individual or class action lawsuits.[136]

The CFPB may enforce certain ECOA violations on its own, but it must refer any matter to the DOJ where the Bureau has reason to believe that one or more creditors has engaged in a "pattern or practice" of discouraging or denying applications for credit in violation of Section 701(a) of the ECOA (which contains the ECOA's basic prohibition on discrimination).[137] The CFPB has primary authority to administratively enforce the ECOA against banks with more than $10 billion in assets. The CFPB has authority to commence a lawsuit in federal court if the DOJ declines to pursue the referral or in cases that involve allegations other than discouraging or denying applications. The Dodd-Frank Act requires that the CFPB work together with the FTC,[138] HUD, and the DOJ to coordinate enforcement activities and promote consistent regulatory treatment of consumer financial products and services.

Before the CFPB was established, a bank's prudential regulator was primarily responsible for investigating potential federal ECOA violations. Effective July 2011, the prudential regulators have supervisory and enforcement authority for the ECOA only for banks with less than $10 billion in assets. The prudential regulators have back-up authority to enforce the ECOA for larger banks if the CFPB does not act on a referral from the regulator within 120 days.

Similar to the CFPB's authority under the ECOA, a bank's prudential regulator is required to refer any "pattern or practice" violations of the ECOA to the DOJ where the regulator has reason to believe that one or more creditors engaged in a pattern or practice of discouraging or denying applications for credit.[139] If the DOJ declines to pursue the referral, then the prudential regulator can independently pursue its own ECOA enforcement action against a bank.

2. CFPB Guidance on Same-Sex Marriage and Interpretive Rule Regarding Sexual Orientation and Gender Identity

In response to the U.S. Supreme Court's 2013 decision in *United States v. Windsor*,[140] the CFPB issued guidance designed to ensure equal treatment for legally married same-sex couples.[141] In *Windsor*, the Court held as unconstitutional Section 3 of the Defense of Marriage Act, which defined the word "marriage" as "a legal union between one man and one woman as husband and wife" and the word "spouse" as referring "only to a person of the opposite sex who is a husband or a wife."[142]

The CFPB's guidance states that, regardless of a person's state of residency, the Bureau will consider a person who is married under the laws of any jurisdiction to be married nationwide for purposes of enforcing, administering, or interpreting the statutes, regulations, and policies under the Bureau's jurisdiction (including the ECOA). The CFPB added that it "will not regard a person to be married by virtue

A-4

of being in a domestic partnership, civil union, or other relationship not denominated by law as a marriage."[143]

In 2020, the U.S. Supreme Court ruled in *Bostock v. Clayton County, Georgia* that the prohibition against sex discrimination in Title VII of the Civil Rights Act of 1964 encompasses both sexual orientation discrimination and gender identity discrimination.[144] In the wake of the *Bostock* decision, the CFPB issued an interpretive rule in 2021 clarifying that the ECOA's prohibition against sex discrimination includes a prohibition against discrimination on the basis of sexual orientation, gender identity, or actual or perceived nonconformity with traditional sex- or gender-based stereotypes.[145] The Bureau issued its interpretive rule to address any regulatory uncertainty that may still have existed under the ECOA and Regulation B after the *Bostock* opinion as to the term "sex" to ensure fair, equitable, and nondiscriminatory access to credit for both individuals and communities and to ensure that consumers are protected from discrimination.

B. Fair Housing Act

The FHAct was enacted in 1968 as Title VIII of the Civil Rights Act. The Civil Rights Act of 1968 was signed into law after a lengthy struggle in Congress to pass the legislation. President Lyndon Johnson leveraged the national tragedy of Reverend Martin Luther King, Jr.'s assassination to urge Congress to finally approve the bill. President Johnson viewed the Civil Rights Act as a fitting memorial to Dr. King's life work, and he desired that the legislation be passed prior to Dr. King's funeral in Atlanta, Georgia. Congress passed the legislation, which included the FHAct, only six days after Dr. King's death.

The purpose of the FHAct is to prohibit discrimination in all aspects of the sale, rental, or financing of a dwelling (known as a "residential real estate-related transaction") on a prohibited basis. The prohibited bases under the FHAct are:

FHAct Prohibited Bases
<ul><li>Race</li><li>National origin</li><li>Color</li><li>Religion</li><li>Sex (including sexual orientation and gender identity)</li><li>Handicap[146]</li><li>Familial status (defined as children under the age of 18 living with a parent or legal custodian, pregnant persons, and people securing custody of children under 18)</li></ul>

The FHAct is primarily enforced by HUD, which maintains rulemaking authority, but the DOJ and the prudential regulators also share enforcement authority.[147] Each prudential regulator is required to forward any facts or information to HUD alleging violations of FHAct that arise through receipt of a consumer complaint, an examination, or other means. If such facts or information indicate a possible pattern or practice of discrimination in violation of the FHAct, then the prudential regulator must also forward the facts or information to the DOJ.[148]

1. FHAct Supervisory and Enforcement Authority

HUD may pursue FHAct actions on its own or work with the prudential regulators and the CFPB to address them. A regulator must refer a matter to the DOJ if it has evidence that a bank engaged in a possible pattern or practice of discrimination in violation of the FHAct. On its own initiative, the DOJ may also bring an action in federal court whenever it "has reasonable cause to believe that any person or group of persons is engaged in a pattern or practice" that violated the FHAct or that "any group of persons has been denied any rights [under the FHAct] and such denial raises an issue of general public importance."[149] The prudential regulators have supervisory and enforcement authority for enforcing the FHAct for all banks.

An individual alleging a FHAct violation may file a complaint with HUD.[150] Upon the filing of a complaint, a HUD investigator will determine whether there is enough evidence to support an FHAct claim. If there is sufficient evidence, the HUD investigator will give the parties an opportunity to pursue voluntary conciliation. If one or both parties refuse to conciliate, HUD conducts an investigation and determines whether there is probable cause to commence administrative proceedings. In addition to investigating individual consumer complaints, the HUD Secretary may initiate his/her own investigations.[151] HUD can either determine liability through its own administrative process or refer the matter to the DOJ upon election of any party to the action. Complainants may also file a private lawsuit on their own behalf.

2. HUD's Rules and Guidance on Sexual Orientation and Gender Identity

In January 2012, HUD issued a final rule (known as the "equal access" rule), which amended its regulations to prohibit discrimination based on actual or perceived sexual orientation or gender identity in regard to mortgage loans insured by the Federal Housing Administration.[152] Following the U.S. Supreme Court's *Bostock* decision in 2020, President Biden issued an Executive Order in January 2021 stating that laws that prohibit sex discrimination, like the FHAct, also should be interpreted to prohibit discrimination on the basis of gender identity and sexual orientation.[153] The following month, HUD issued a Memorandum concluding that the Fair Housing Act's sex discrimination provisions were comparable to those of Title VII and that they likewise prohibit discrimination based on sexual orientation and gender identity.[154] The Memorandum further directed HUD's Office of Fair Housing and Equal Opportunity to fully enforce the FHAct to prohibit such discrimination.

In 2021, HUD began enforcing the prohibition sex discrimination under the FHAct as including both sexual orientation and gender identity. For example, in 2022, HUD entered into a settlement agreement with a company based on allegations that it discriminated against a transgender woman and her family in the terms, conditions, or privileges of the rental of a dwelling when the company gave written notice to the complainant to act and dress like a man.[155]

3.   HUD's Disparate Impact Rulemaking

In February 2013, HUD issued a final rule that codified its standards for disparate impact claims brought under the FHAct. Under this rule, once a lender's practice has been shown by the plaintiff to have a disparate impact on a protected class, the lender would then have the burden of showing that the challenged practice "is necessary to achieve one or more substantial, legitimate, nondiscriminatory interests."[156] This second step is different than the traditional test used by courts, as explained in Chapter III. Even if the lender can satisfy this burden, under the rule, courts can find that the lender violated the FHAct if another practice could serve the same purpose with less discriminatory effect.

In 2015, the U.S. Supreme Court issued its ruling in *Texas Department of Housing and Community Affairs v. Inclusive Communities Project,*[157] concluding that Congress intended the FHAct to permit disparate impact claims based on its interpretation of the FHAct's text, the amendment history of the FHAct, and the purpose of the FHAct.

A-8

Therefore, the Court held that a defendant may be liable under the FHAct for a policy or practice that has an adverse impact on members of a particular protected class group.

The Court did not address HUD's disparate impact rule in its *Inclusive Communities* opinion, but instead focused on the three-step, burden-shifting framework used by the courts to prove disparate impact claims by clarifying its interpretation of that framework.[158] The burden-shifting framework described by the Supreme Court differed from the version of the burden-shifting test contained in HUD's disparate impact rule, resulting in subsequent uncertainty and legal challenges.

As a result, in September 2020, HUD adopted a final rule amending its 2013 disparate impact standard regulation to better reflect the Supreme Court's ruling in *Inclusive Communities* and to establish a uniform standard for determining when a housing policy or practice with discriminatory effect violates the FHAct.[159] This new rule utilizes a five-prong test to assess claims of disparate impact and adds new defenses to such claims. Although the rule was supposed to go into effect in October 2020, a federal court enjoined its implementation. Then in June 2021, HUD published a proposal to rescind the 2020 disparate impact rule and replace it with the original 2013 rule. On March 17, 2023, HUD finally issued its final rule re-adopting the agency's 2013 disparate impact standards.

The Supreme Court's decision in *Inclusive Communities* and HUD's re-adoption of the 2013 formulation of its disparate impact rule is expected to embolden government agencies and private plaintiffs to continue to assert claims of disparate impact discrimination under the FHAct and the ECOA. Therefore, it is advisable for banks to examine new and existing policies, procedures, and business practices for the potential risk of disparate impact and take steps to reduce fair lending risk. This may include modifying or discontinuing the policy or practice, or reaching a satisfactory conclusion that the policy/practice does not in fact cause disparate impact by using the Supreme Court's approach to the three-step test.

C.   Community Reinvestment Act

The CRA was enacted in 1977 to encourage banks to lend to the entire community from which banks drew deposits – specifically, to provide credit to residents of low- and moderate-income neighborhoods in their local communities. The CRA is not a fair lending law because it does not by itself prohibit discriminatory conduct based on race, ethnicity or membership in any other protected class, but it supports the objectives of the fair lending laws.

The CRA is enforced by the prudential regulators, and those regulators each issue their own rules implementing the CRA. Although the prudential regulators successfully coordinated a major update of their CRA rules in 1995 by working together collaboratively to align them, efforts in recent years to revise and modernize each agency's CRA rules have not gone as smoothly. After interagency CRA rulemaking efforts fell apart in 2019, the OCC issued its own final rule in 2020, which was then rescinded in 2021 during the Biden administration. The OCC, FRB, and FDIC then began working together again to attempt to achieve consensus in their approach to revamping each agency's CRA rules. On May 5, 2022, the OCC, FRB, and FDIC issued a notice of joint proposed rulemaking that would, among other things, expand access to credit, investment, and basic banking services in low- and moderate-income communities, adapt to changes in the banking industry, and provide greater clarity, consistency, and transparency.[160] Comments were due on August 6, 2022, and a final rule is expected in 2023.

It is important to note that fair lending and CRA performance are linked in the examination process. The prudential regulators examine and rate a bank's compliance with the CRA. A bank that violates the fair lending laws and regulations can be subject to a CRA ratings downgrade by its examining agency and can face restrictions on its ability to engage in certain business activities, including opening a new branch or entering into a merger or acquisition.

The CRA does not give government agencies or private individuals a statutory cause of action against banks. Nevertheless, the CRA has become increasingly tied to fair lending as regulators find fault with banks' long-standing self-designated CRA assessment areas and use it as proof of discrimination in redlining enforcement actions. In addition, private litigants have supported their fair lending claims by alleging that a bank failed to meet its CRA obligations.

D.   Home Mortgage Disclosure Act

HMDA, which is implemented by Regulation C, requires certain mortgage lenders to collect and report to federal regulators, and disclose to the public, certain data about mortgage loan applications and originations, including the race, national origin and gender of loan applicants.[161] On an annual basis, lenders must disclose all of the information specified in Regulation C, commonly referred to as "HMDA data" to the appropriate federal government agency, which the FFIEC then aggregates and makes available to the public (typically each September).

Regulation C contains an Official Staff Commentary (Supplement I to 12 C.F.R. Part 1003), initially issued by the FRB and subsequently adopted by the CFPB, which further interprets HMDA's requirements. Additional guidance on HMDA data collecting and reporting requirements can be found in *A Guide to HMDA Reporting: Getting It Right!*[162] *See* Chapter VIII for more information.

HMDA is not a fair lending law, but government agencies use HMDA data as an initial screening mechanism for fair lending examinations to determine mortgage lending risk areas. Furthermore, federal regulators, consumer advocacy groups, and private litigants rely primarily on HMDA data when claiming that a bank did not apply its mortgage lending policies or practices equally to similarly situated applicants or borrowers. For instance, a plaintiff could develop a regression model using HMDA data to identify potential disparities in loan pricing for minority borrowers versus non-minority borrowers. However, it is important to recognize that HMDA data provide an incomplete – and potentially misleading – picture of a lender's underwriting and pricing practices.

In recent years, the federal regulators — and the CFPB in particular — have emphasized the importance of accurate HMDA data. The CFPB has brought 5 HMDA enforcement actions – two of which involved significant civil money penalties since 2013. *See* Chapter XIII for more information on these enforcement actions. [163]

E.   Unfair, Deceptive, and Abusive Acts or Practices

Federal regulators, enforcement agencies and consumer advocacy groups have consistently focused on the need for banks to be more accountable for engaging in responsible lending. Responsible lending emphasizes economic and procedural fairness and transparency in dealing with consumers, including, among other things, providing clear, balanced and understandable terms and conditions, allowing consumers to make informed choices, refraining from taking unfair advantage of vulnerable consumer populations, and ensuring that financial products

A-12

and services provide value to consumers commensurate with the costs.[164]

Responsible lending concepts are based primarily on violations of the federal unfair or deceptive acts or practices laws. Specifically, Section 5 of the FTC Act prohibits engaging in "unfair or deceptive acts of practices" ("UDAP")[165] and sections 1031 and 1036 of the Dodd-Frank Act prohibits unfair, deceptive, and abusive acts or practices ("UDAAP").[166] The FTC has responsibility for interpreting and enforcing UDAP, and the CFPB has responsibility for interpreting and enforcing UDAAP. Both agencies have used their powers expansively. In addition, all 50 states and the District of Columbia have their own UDAP laws that can be enforced by the state attorney general and, in some instances, through a private right of action.

Unlike Section 5 of the FTC Act, the Dodd-Frank Act prohibits "abusive" acts or practices. For several years, the CFPB avoided specifying the meaning of "abusive" and instead referred to the definition of the term in the Dodd-Frank Act and used enforcement actions to define the term on a case-by-case basis.[167]

In 2020, the CFPB, under the leadership of Director Kathleen Kraninger, issued a policy statement recognizing that there was uncertainty as to the scope and meaning of "abusiveness."[168] The policy statement stated that an act or practice is not abusive unless it: "(1) materially interferes with the ability of a consumer to understand a term or condition of a consumer financial product or service; or (2) takes unreasonable advantage of— (A) a lack of understanding on the part of the consumer of the material risks, costs, or conditions of the product or service; (B) the inability of the consumer to protect the interests of the consumer in selecting or using a consumer financial product or service; or (C) the reasonable reliance by the consumer on a covered person to act in the interests of the consumer." In addition, the CFPB stated that (1) it intended to cite conduct as abusive if the harms to consumers from the conduct outweigh the benefits to the consumers, (2) the Bureau would avoid challenging conduct as both abusive and unfair or deceptive, and (3) that the Bureau would not seek certain types of monetary relief for violations of the abusiveness standard where the covered person was making a good faith effort to comply with the abusiveness standard.[169]

In March 2021, the CFPB reversed course under Director Rohit Chopra, rescinding its policy statement on abusive acts and practices.[170] The CFPB stated that the 2020 policy statement undermined deterrence and was contrary to its mission of protecting consumers. The CFPB then issued a new policy statement in April 2023 defining abusive practices, providing a new framework for abusive practices, as interpreted by Director Chopra, and reinstituting penalties for non-compliance.[171]

Since 2011, the CFPB has undertaken enforcement actions based on alleged violations of UDAAP alone and also alleged UDAAP violations where the Bureau finds a violation of other consumer financial protection laws. At this point, there are no signs that the CFPB will stop using its UDAAP enforcement authority expansively. In fact, as discussed in the following section, the CFPB is actively seeking to broadly expand its interpretation of UDAAP in an unprecedented manner.

It is important to note that responsible banking laws — such as UDAAP — and fair lending laws often intersect because both concepts involve the unfair treatment of consumers. For example, an unclear disclosure about the fees charged for a particular loan may disproportionately affect members of a protected class and result in substantial injury to affected consumers.

A-14

1. The CFPB's Massive Expansion of UDAAP Through Revisions to its UDAAP Examination Manual

In 2022, the CFPB seized upon the complementary nature of UDAAP and fair lending concepts by issuing a press release announcing significant revisions to its UDAAP Examination Manual ("Manual") and indicating that discrimination is now actionable under the "unfair" prong of UDAAP.[172]

Although not explicitly mentioned by the CFPB, the updated UDAAP Examination Manual strongly indicates that the CFPB plans to use both disparate treatment and disparate impact analyses as a way of establishing "unfair" discrimination. For example, the Manual urges Bureau examiners to consider whether a supervised entity has "a process to take prompt corrective action if the decision-making processes it uses produce deficiencies or discriminatory results."[173] Further, examiners must consider whether a supervised entity ensures that employees and third-party service providers "refrain from engaging in servicing or collection practices that lead to differential treatment or disproportionately adverse impacts on a discriminatory basis."[174] This appears to signal that the CFPB believes that the disparate impact doctrine now applies to every aspect of every financial services provider over which the Bureau has jurisdiction.

By expanding the reach of its unfair practices authority to include discrimination, the CFPB now has the power to examine potentially discriminatory practices in both new markets and involving activities outside of its authority under the ECOA. Under the ECOA, discrimination is prohibited only against "applicants" for credit. In its press release, the CFPB specifically noted that it would examine for discrimination in "all consumer finance markets," including non-credit products like payments, consumer reporting, remittances, and deposit accounts.[175]

In addition, the CFPB specifically highlighted targeted marketing, which typically is considered to be outside of the scope of the ECOA because viewers of advertisements are not "applicants." The updated UDAAP Examination Manual states that transaction testing should determine whether a supervised entity "engages in targeted advertising or marketing in a discriminatory way." The Manual also notes that a supervised entity's policies, procedures, and practices should "not target or exclude consumers from products and services, or offer different terms and conditions, in a discriminatory manner." Now, for the first time, the CFPB has explicitly asserted that targeted marketing is discriminatory or actionable, although how the Bureau intends to assess targeted advertising remains unclear. Nevertheless, the Bureau's revised Manual clearly signaled that the Bureau will examine targeted advertising.

In response to the CFPB's extraordinary policy action to expand its interpretation of UDAAP, the U.S. Chamber of Commerce, American Bankers Association, Consumer Bankers Association, and three other trade groups filed a lawsuit against the Bureau in September 2022 challenging the CFPB's UDAAP Examination Manual modifications. *See* Complaint, *Chamber of Commerce of the U.S.A. v. Consumer Financial Protection Bureau*, No. 6:22-cv-00381-JCB (E.D. Tex., Sept. 28, 2022). The plaintiffs claim that the modifications should be disallowed because (1) the update exceeds the CFPB's authority under the Dodd-Frank Act because the Act only grants the CFPB authority to enforce anti-discrimination principles in certain circumstances; (2) the update is arbitrary and capricious; (3) the CFPB did not follow the Administrative Procedures Act's notice and comment rulemaking procedures in adopting these sweeping policy changes; and (4) the update should be discarded because the CFPB's funding structure violates the Appropriations Clause of the U.S. Constitution. Notably, in October 2022, the Fifth Circuit Court of Appeals held that the funding mechanism for the CFPB is unconstitutional because the CFPB does not receive its funding from annual Congressional appropriations. Unsurprisingly, defendants in enforcement actions are citing this decision as a basis for dismissal of the lawsuits brought against them and the CFPB has argued that the holding is neither controlling nor correct. The constitutionality of the CFPB's funding is likely to continue to be a significant issue in 2023.

In light of this significant CFPB development, as you oversee your bank's fair lending program in your role as a bank director, it will be important to revisit your bank's fair lending program to ensure that it encompasses compliance monitoring and testing that addresses this new concept of discrimination as UDAAP.

APPENDIX B: REGULATORY REFERENCE MATERIALS

Regulatory Guidance

Key Fair Lending Regulatory Guidance

- *Joint Policy Statement on Discrimination in Lending*, 59 Fed. Reg. 18267 (Apr. 15, 1994)
- FDIC FIL 36-96 – *Side-by-Side: A Guide to Fair Lending* (June 6, 1996)
- CFPB Bulletin 2012-04 (Fair Lending), *Lending Discrimination* (Apr. 18, 2012)
- CFPB, White Paper, *Using Publicly Available Information to Proxy for Unidentified Race and Ethnicity* (Summer 2014)
- Memorandum from Eric Holder, Attorney General of the United States, to the President Barack Obama, "Implementation of *United States v. Windsor*" (June 20, 2014)
- Memorandum from Richard Cordray, Director of the Consumer Financial Protection Bureau, to CFPB Staff, "Ensuring Equal Treatment for Same-Sex Married Couples" (June 25, 2014)
- *Equal Access to Housing in HUD Programs Regardless of Sexual Orientation or Gender Identity*, 77 Fed. Reg. 5662 (Feb. 3, 2012); 24 C.F.R. § 5.105(a)(2)
- Presidential Executive Order No. 13988, 86 Fed. Reg. 7023, "Preventing and Combatting Discrimination on the Basis of Gender Identity or Sexual Orientation" (Jan. 20, 2021)
- Memorandum from Jeanine M. Worden, Acting Assistant Secretary for Fair Housing & Equal Opportunity, to the Office of Fair Housing & Equal Opportunity, Fair Housing Assistance Program Agencies, Fair Housing Initiatives Program Grantees, "Implementation of Executive Order 13988 on the Enforcement of the Fair Housing Act" (Feb. 11, 2021)
- CFPB, *Advisory Opinion on Special Purpose Credit Programs* (Dec. 21, 2020)

- HUD, *Office of General Counsel Guidance on the Fair Housing Act's Treatment of Certain Special Purpose Credit Programs That Are Designed and Implemented in Compliance with the Equal Credit Opportunity Act and Regulation B* (Dec. 6, 2021)
- OCC, Bulletin 2022-3, *Fair Lending: Interagency Statement on Special Purpose Credit Programs* (Feb. 22, 2022)
- Fair Housing Finance Agency, *Fair Lending Policy Statement,* 86 Fed. Reg. 36199, (July 9, 2021)
- HUD, *Reinstatement of Discriminatory Effects Standard*, 88 Fed. Reg. 19450, **(**Mar. 31, 2023) [codified at 24 C.F.R. pt. 100]

Key HMDA Regulatory Guidance

- CFPB Bulletin 2013-11, "Home Mortgage Disclosure Act (HMDA) and Regulation C – Compliance Management; CFPB HMDA Resubmission Schedule and Guidelines; and HMDA Enforcement" (Oct. 9, 2013)
- CFPB, *Status of New Uniform Residential Loan Application and Collection of Expanded Home Mortgage Disclosure Act Information about Ethnicity and Race in 2017 under Regulation B* (Sept. 23, 2016)
- CFPB, *Reportable HMDA Data: A Regulatory and Reporting Overview Reference Chart for HMDA Data Collected in 2022* (Jan. 1, 2022), https://files.consumerfinance.gov/f/documents/2022_cfpb_reportable-hmda-data_regulatory-and-reporting-overview-reference-chart.pdf
- FFIEC, *A Guide to HMDA Reporting: Getting it Right!* (2022)

Key Responsible Lending Guidance

- FTC, Policy Statement on Unfairness (Dec. 17, 1980)
- FTC, Policy Statement on Deception (Oct. 14, 1983)
- CFPB, Bulletin 2012-06, *Marketing of Credit Card Add-On Products* (July 18, 2012)

- CFPB, Bulletin 2013-07, *Prohibition of Unfair, Deceptive, or Abusive Acts or Practices in the Collection of Consumer Debts* (July 10, 2013)
- FFIEC, *Interagency Guidance Regarding Unfair or Deceptive Credit Practices* (Aug. 22, 2014)
- CFPB, Bulletin 2014-02, *Marketing of Credit Card Promotional APR Offers* (Sept. 3, 2014)
- CFPB, Bulletin 2017-01, *Phone Pay Fees* (July 27, 2017)
- CFPB, Statement of Policy Regarding Prohibition on Abusive Acts or Practices (Jan. 24, 2020)
- CFPB, Statement of Policy Regarding Prohibition on Abusive Acts or Practices; Rescission (Mar. 11, 2021)
- CFPB, Bulletin 2022-04: *Mitigating Harm from Repossession of Automobiles* (Feb. 28, 2022)
- CFPB, Bulletin 2022-06: *Unfair Returned Deposited Item Fee Assessment Practices* (Oct. 26, 2022)
- CFPB, Policy Statement on Abusive Practices, 88 Fed. Reg. 21883 (Apr. 12, 2023)

Key CRA Regulatory Guidance

The prudential regulators periodically issue CRA questions and answers, which are valuable to the banking industry in understanding how examiners will apply the CRA and related rules, and the FFIEC maintains a repository of CRA interpretive letters. Both are noted below:

- OCC, FRB & FDIC, *Community Reinvestment Act; Interagency Questions and Answers Regarding Community Reinvestment; Notice,* (81 Fed. Reg. 48506, July 25, 2016)
- FFIEC, CRA Interpretive Letters, available by year at https://www.ffiec.gov/cra/letters.htm

Among the prudential regulators, the OCC tends to issue the most guidance on the CRA, and recent examples can be found below:

- OCC Bulletin 2018-23, *Community Reinvestment Act: Revisions to Impact of Evidence of Discriminatory or Other Illegal Credit Practices on Community Reinvestment Act Ratings* (Aug. 15, 2018)
- OCC Bulletin 2019-39, *Community Reinvestment Act: Guidelines for Requesting Approval of a Strategic Plan* (July 31, 2019)
- OCC Bulletin 2019-40, *Community Reinvestment Act: Guidelines for Requesting Designation as a Wholesale, Limited Purpose, or Special Purpose Bank* (July 31, 2019)
- OCC Bulletin 2021-12, *Community Reinvestment Act: Interagency Frequently Asked Questions Related to the COVID-19 Pandemic* (Mar. 8, 2021)
- OCC Bulletin 2021-67, *Community Reinvestment Act: Revision of Small and Intermediate Small Bank and Savings Association Asset Thresholds* (Dec. 30, 2021)
- OCC Bulletin 2022-2, *State Community Reinvestment Laws; Consumer Complaints: Input from State Officials and Consumer Complaint Referrals from States* (Feb. 2, 2022)
- OCC Bulletin 2022-4, *Community Reinvestment Act: Frequently Asked Questions Regarding the Final Rule to Rescind the OCC's June 2020 CRA Rule* (Feb. 22, 2021)

Examination Procedures

Fair Lending Examination Procedures

- FFIEC Interagency Fair Lending Examination Procedures (Aug. 2009)
- OCC Comptroller's Handbook – Fair Lending (Jan. 2023)
- CFPB Supervision and Examination Manual – Equal Credit Opportunity Act (ECOA) Procedures (Oct. 2015)
- FRB Consumer Compliance Handbook, V. Federal Fair Lending Regulations and Statutes (Dec. 2016)

- CFPB Supervision and Examination Manual – Equal Credit Opportunity Act (ECOA) Baseline Review Procedures (Apr. 2019)
- FDIC Compliance Examination Manual, IV. Fair Lending Laws and Regulations (March 2021)

HMDA Examination Procedures

- CFPB Supervision and Examination Manual – Home Mortgage Disclosure Act (Apr. 2019)
- FDIC Consumer Compliance Examination Manual – Home Mortgage Disclosure Act (July 2021)
- FRB HMDA Examination Procedures (Nov. 2021)
- OCC Comptroller's Handbook – Home Mortgage Disclosure (Dec. 2021)

UDAP/UDAAP Examination Procedures

- CFPB Supervision and Examination Manual – Unfair, Deceptive, or Abusive Acts or Practices (Mar. 2022)
- FRB Consumer Compliance Handbook, IV. Federal Trade Commission Act Section 5: Unfair or Deceptive Acts or Practices (Dec. 2016)
- OCC Consumer Compliance – Unfair or Deceptive Acts or Practices and Unfair, Deceptive, or Abusive Acts or Practices (June 2020)
- FDIC Compliance Examination Manual, VII. Abusive Practices (June 2022)

CRA Examination Procedures

- OCC, FRB, FDIC & OTS, Small Institution CRA Examination Procedures (July 2007)
- OCC, FRB, FDIC & OTS, Intermediate Small Institution CRA Examination Procedures (July 2007)
- OCC, FRB & FDIC, Large Institution CRA Examination Procedures OCC, FRB, and FDIC (Apr. 2014)
- OCC, FRB, FDIC & OTS, Wholesale/Limited Purpose CRA Examination Procedures (July 2007)

- OCC, FRB, FDIC & OTS, Strategic Plan CRA Examination Procedures (July 2007)
- FRB Consumer Compliance Handbook, VI. Community Reinvestment Act (Dec. 2016)
- OCC, Comptroller's Handbook: Community Reinvestment Act Examination Procedures (Sept. 2019)
- FDIC Compliance Examination Manual, XI. Community Reinvestment Act (March 2022)

ABOUT THE AUTHORS

David Baris is the President of the American Association of Bank Directors ("AABD"). He has led AABD since its founding in 1989. The AABD's mission is to provide bank directors the resources with which to serve their institutions effectively and in a manner that minimizes the risk of personal liability consistent with safe and sound banking practices.

AABD supports bank directors through its advocacy, information, and training initiatives.

Its advocacy efforts include outreach to the federal and state banking agencies; the U.S. Congress and its banking committees and members; the Executive Branch, and the judiciary.

Its information and training initiatives include the establishment of the Institute for Bank Director Education, which supports the Bank Director Certification Program; Core Courses and other training for individual board members; AABD Committees that focus on specific categories of knowledge relevant to bank directors; the Task Force on mitigating the risk of personal liability of bank directors consistent with safe and sound banking; and periodic surveys that allow bank directors to benchmark their efforts.

Mr. Baris is the author of seven books and numerous articles on bank director issues. His books include FDIC Director Suits: Lessons Learned; Bank Director Standards of Care and Protections: A Fifty-State Survey; Bank Director Regulatory Burden Report; and Bank Founder's Guidebook.

Mr. Baris was a banking law partner with several law firms for many years. He also served as Counsel to an oversight subcommittee of the House Government Operations Committee and Legislative Counsel to a Member of Congress. In addition, Mr. Baris was a director at Mutual of Omaha, serving on its Executive, Investment, and Audit Committees.

Lori Sommerfield is a seasoned consumer financial services attorney with over 20 years of experience in federal government, in-house, and private practice settings. She has deep expertise in fair lending and responsible banking regulatory compliance, and she counsels clients in supervisory issues, examinations, investigations, and enforcement actions.

Ms. Sommerfield specializes in the full suite of anti-discrimination laws, including the Equal Credit Opportunity Act, the Fair Housing Act, UDAP/UDAAP, and the Americans with Disabilities Act. She advises clients on traditional areas of fair lending risk and provides legal advice on fair lending statistical analyses and complex predictive data analytics, including artificial intelligence and machine learning models and variables. Ms. Sommerfield also provides advice on designing and implementing effective fair lending and responsible banking risk management programs, and built and managed such a program for a major national bank in a prior role. In addition, she has successfully defended fair lending investigations and enforcement actions by the CFPB and the U.S. Department of Justice throughout her career.

Prior to joining the firm, Ms. Sommerfield held significant positions as in-house counsel at major financial institutions, and she served as outside counsel for financial services clients with two nationally recognized law firms. She began her career as a staff attorney at the FDIC in Washington, D.C., helping formulate bank consumer protection and safety and soundness policies and regulations.

Ms. Sommerfield is an original co-author of the first edition of the Practical Handbook on Fair Lending for Bank Directors and Executive Officers, has contributed fair lending chapters to several legal treatises, and has written numerous legal articles. She speaks frequently at industry and legal conferences and contributes regularly to Troutman Pepper's client webinars, podcasts and blog posts.

Chris Willis is the co-leader of the Consumer Financial Services Regulatory Practice at Troutman Pepper. For more than 25 years, Mr. Willis has counseled clients in the consumer financial services industry in the areas of compliance, enforcement, examinations, and litigation. He advises financial services institutions facing state and federal government investigations and examinations, counseling them on compliance issues including fair lending, UDAP/UDAAP, credit reporting, and debt collection, and defending them in individual and class action lawsuits brought by consumers and enforcement actions brought by government agencies.

Mr. Willis also leverages insights from his enforcement and litigation experience to help clients design new products and processes, including machine learning marketing, fraud prevention and underwriting models, product structure, advertising, online application flows, underwriting, and collection and loss mitigation strategies.

Mr. Willis brings a highly practical focus to his legal advice, informed by balancing a deep understanding of the business of consumer finance and the practical priorities of federal and state regulatory agencies.

Mr. Willis speaks frequently at conferences across the U.S. on consumer financial services law and has been featured in numerous articles in publications such as the *Wall Street Journal*, the *New York Times*, the *Washington Post*, *American Banker*, *National Law Journal*, *BNA Bloomberg*, and *Bank Safety and Soundness Advisor*.

Sarah Pruett, an associate at Troutman Pepper, defends and advises banks, fintechs, and other financial services companies in complex legal matters involving state and federal government investigations, enforcement proceedings, and individual and class action lawsuits pertaining to state and federal consumer protection laws and fraud. Her proficiency in litigation and enforcement matters extends to e-discovery, where she has gained significant experience in negotiating with opposing counsel and government regulators to limit the scope and burden of subpoenas and civil investigative demands. Ms. Pruett also provides guidance to clients on compliance with consumer finance laws and regulations, ensuring they operate within the bounds of the law.

With a focus on consumer financial services, Ms. Pruett has extensive experience defending her clients in matters related to the Fair Credit Reporting Act, Fair Debt Collection Practices Act, Equal Credit Opportunity Act, Truth in Lending Act, UDAP/UDAAP, state consumer protection laws, and fraud. She is well-versed in representing clients facing investigations and enforcement proceedings brought by key agencies such as the Consumer Financial Protection Bureau, the Federal Trade Commission, and various state agencies. Her areas of experience include auto finance, short-term lending, fair lending, debt collection, credit reporting, payment processing, and UDAAP issues.

Prior to joining Troutman Pepper, was an associate at two national law firms, representing clients in complex commercial litigation and regulatory enforcement matters.

Ms. Pruett obtained her J.D. degree from Cornell Law School, graduating *cum laude*. While attending law school, she contributed to the *Cornell Law Review*. She is admitted to practice law in New York and Minnesota. In addition to co-authoring the 2nd edition of the Fair Lending Handbook, Ms. Pruett is a co-author of the Fair Lending chapter in the American Bar Association's Consumer Financial Services Treatise. *The Best Lawyers in America* recognized Ms. Pruett as "Ones to Watch" in 2022.

TROUTMAN PEPPER

Troutman Pepper Hamilton Sanders LLP ("Troutman Pepper") is a national law firm with more than 1,200 attorneys strategically located in 23 U.S. cities. The firm's regulatory, litigation, and transactional practices advise a diverse client base, from start-ups to multinational enterprises. The firm provides sophisticated legal solutions to clients' most pressing business challenges, with significant depth across industry sectors, including financial services, energy, health sciences, insurance, and private equity, among others.

Troutman Pepper's nationally known Consumer Financial Services practice represents bank and non-bank clients in a wide range of regulatory and dispute resolution issues involving consumer finance laws. The firm's Fair Lending team covers the full range of issues arising out of the Equal Credit Opportunity Act and the Fair Housing Act, as well as state and local fair lending and anti-discrimination laws. This national team includes attorneys with significant experience in defending fair lending investigations and enforcement actions by the CFPB, the DOJ, the federal banking regulators, HUD, and state attorneys general, as well as fair lending-focused examinations by the CFPB, OCC, FDIC, Federal Reserve Board, and the New York Department of Financial Services.

ENDNOTES

[1]   12 U.S.C. § 5481(13).

[2]   In the past, responsible lending largely focused on compliance with unfair or deceptive acts or practices law under Section 5 of the Federal Trade Commission Act, state anti-predatory lending laws, and the Home Ownership and Equity Protection Act ("HOEPA"), which places limits on high-cost mortgage loans. In recent years, responsible lending laws have been expanded to include the unfair, deceptive, or abusive acts or practices ("UDAAP") under the Dodd-Frank Act and the Servicemembers Civil Relief Act ("SCRA"). Responsible lending is often viewed as a complementary concept to fair lending, but it is only addressed tangentially in this book.

[3]   U.S. DEP'T OF JUSTICE, ATTORNEY GENERAL'S 2014 ANNUAL REPORT TO CONGRESS PURSUANT TO THE EQUAL CREDIT OPPORTUNITY ACT AMENDMENTS OF 1976 (2015).

[4]   U.S. Dep't of Justice, Attorney General's 2020 Annual Report to Congress Pursuant to the Equal Credit Opportunity Act Amendments of 1976 (2021).

[5]   Consent Order, *United States v. Countrywide Fin. Corp.*, No. 2:11-cv-10540-PSG-AJW (C.D. Cal. Dec. 28, 2011).

[6]   Consent Order, *United States v. Wells Fargo Bank, NA*, No. 1:12-cv-01150-JDB (D.D.C. Sept. 21, 2012).

[7]   Press Release, Dep't of Justice, Justice Department Announces New Initiative to Combat Redlining (Oct. 22, 2021).

[8]   Consent Order, *United States v. Trustmark Nat'l Bank*, No. 2:21-cv-2664 (W.D. Tenn., Oct. 27, 2021) (requiring a $3.85 million loan subsidy program and $5 million civil penalty); Consent Order, *United States v. Bancorpsouth Bank*, No. 1:16cv118 (N.D. Miss. July 25, 2016).

[9]   *See* Consent Order, *Ally Fin. Inc. & Ally Bank*, CFPB No. 2013-CFPB-0010 (Dec. 20, 2013) [hereinafter CFPB Ally Consent Order]. Creditors are prohibited under Regulation B from inquiring about a borrower's race, ethnicity, or gender in connection with non-mortgage loan applications. The federal government has adopted various methodologies to predict a person's race or ethnicity in non-mortgage lending investigations in order to determine which borrowers are prohibited basis group members.

[10]   In the event that an auto dealer charges the consumer an interest rate that is higher than the lender's buy rate, the lender may pay the auto dealer what is typically referred to as dealer "reserve" or "participation" — compensation based upon the difference in interest revenues between the buy rate and the actual note rate charged to the consumer in the retail installment contract executed with the dealer, or a percentage of that difference where the dealer and lender split the amount (*e.g.*, 50/50, 60/40, etc.). Dealer reserve is one method indirect auto lenders use to compensate

dealers for the value they add by originating loans and finding financing sources. The exact computation of compensation based on dealer mark-up varies across lenders and may even vary among programs at the same lender.

[11]   Consent Order, *United States v. Synchrony Bank*, No. 2:14-CV-00454-DS (D. Utah June 27, 2014); Consent Order, *In the Matter of: Synchrony Bank, f/k/a GE Capital Retail Bank*, CFPB No. 2014-CFPB-0007 (June 19, 2014) [hereinafter CFPB Synchrony Bank Consent Order].

[12]   Consent Order, *Am. Express Centurion Bank*, No. 2017-CFPB-0016 (Aug. 23, 2017).

[13]   Agreed Order, *United States v. Luther Burbank Sav.*, No. 2:12-cv-07809-JAK-FMO (C.D. Cal. Oct. 12, 2012).

[14]   Consent Order, *Cmty. First Bank Pikesville, Md.*, No. AA-EC-2012-124, OCC No. 2013-025 (Mar. 18, 2013).

[15]   268 F.R.D. 627 (N.D. Cal. 2010).

[16]   *See* NAT'L FAIR HOUS. ALLIANCE, ZIP CODE INEQUALITY: DISCRIMINATION BY BANKS IN THE MAINTENANCE OF HOMES IN NEIGHBORHOODS OF COLOR (2014); NAT'L FAIR HOUS. ALLIANCE, THE BANKS ARE BACK – OUR NEIGHBORHOODS ARE NOT: DISCRIMINATION IN THE MAINTENANCE AND MARKETING OF REO PROPERTIES (2012); NAT'L FAIR HOUS. ALLIANCE, HERE COMES THE BANK, THERE GOES THE NEIGHBORHOOD (2011).

[17]   Conciliation Agreement, between U.S. Dep't of Hous. & Urban Dev. and Wells Fargo Bank, N.A., HUD No. 00-13-0001-8 (June 5, 2013).

[18]   Press Release, Nat'l Fair Hous. Alliance, Mortgage Giant Fannie Mae Accused of Racial Discrimination in 34 U.S. Metro Areas (May 13, 2015).

[19]   *See, e.g.*, Press Release, Nat'l Fair Hous. Alliance, Bank of America Charged with Creating Unhealthy Housing Through Widespread Practice of Housing Discrimination (Nov. 14, 2013); Press Release, Nat'l Fair Hous. Alliance, U.S. Bank Accused of Racial Discrimination in Five More Cities (Nov. 18, 2014); Press Release, Nat'l Fair Hous. Alliance, Fannie Mae Contractor Cyprexx Accused of Race Discrimination in Four U.S. Cities (July 22, 2014); Press Release, Nat'l Fair Hous. Alliance, Fannie Mae Contractor Accused of Race Discrimination in Richmond and Three Other U.S. Cities (July 22, 2014). HUD found no violation by U.S. Bank and closed the matter in Jan. 2016.

[20]   *See, e.g.*, Complaint, *City of Miami v. JPMorgan Chase & Co.*, No. 1:14-cv-22205, 2014 WL 2709434 (S.D. Fla. June 13, 2014); First Amended Complaint, *City of Los Angeles v. JPMorgan Chase & Co.*, No. 2:14-cv-04168, 2014 WL 4383509 (C.D. Cal. Aug. 26, 2014); Complaint, *City of Miami v. Wells Fargo & Co.*, No. 1:13-cv-24508 (S.D. Fla. Dec. 13, 2013); Complaint, *City of Miami v. Citigroup Inc.*, No. 1:13-cv-24510 (S.D. Fla. Dec. 13, 2013); Complaint, *City of Miami Gardens v. Wells Fargo & Co.*, No. 1:14-cv-22203 (S.D. Fla. June 13, 2014); Complaint, *City of Miami Gardens v.*

Citigroup Inc., No. 1:14-cv-22204 (S.D. Fla. June 13, 2014); Complaint, *City of Miami Gardens v. JPMorgan Chase & Co.*, No. 1:14-cv-22206 (S.D. Fla. June 13, 2014); Complaint, *City of Miami Gardens v. Bank of Am. Corp.*, No. 1:14-cv-22202 (S.D. Fla. June 13, 2014); Complaint, *City of Los Angeles v. Bank of Am. Corp.*, No. 2:13CV09046, 2013 WL 6502834 (C.D. Cal. Dec. 6, 2013); Complaint, *City of Los Angeles v. Wells Fargo & Co.*, No. 2:13CV09007, 2013 WL 6916826 (C.D. Cal. Dec. 5, 2013); Complaint, *City of Los Angeles v. Citigroup Inc.*, No. 2:13CV09009 (C.D. Cal. Dec. 5, 2013); Complaint, *City of Oakland v. Wells Fargo Bank, N.A.*, No. 3:15-cv-04321 (N.D. Cal. Sept. 21, 2015); Complaint, *DeKalb Cnty. v. HSBC N. Am. Holdings Inc.*, No. 1:12-cv-03640 (N.D. Ga. Oct. 18, 2012); Amended Complaint, *Cnty. of Cook v. HSBC N. Am. Holdings Inc.*, No. 1:14-cv-2031, 2014 WL 1677060 (N.D. Ill. Mar. 31, 2014).

[21]   *See* Remarks of CFPB Director Rohit Chopra at a Joint DOJ, CFPB, and OCC Press Conference on the Trustmark National Bank Enforcement Action (Oct. 22, 2021) ("We should never assume that algorithms will be free of bias. If we want to move toward a society where each of us has equal opportunities, we need to investigate whether discriminatory black box models are undermining that goal.").

[22]   Interagency Statement on the Use of Alternative Data in Credit Underwriting (Dec. 3, 2019) ("As the agencies gain a deeper understanding of alternative data usages, they may offer further information on the appropriate use of alternative data. Firms may choose to consult with appropriate regulators when planning for the use of alternative data."),

[23]   *See* Complaint, *United States v. Meta Platforms, Inc. f/k/a Facebook, Inc.*, No. 1:22-CV-5187 (S.D.N.Y. June 21, 2022) (alleging discrimination in social media targeting for housing-related advertisements, in violation of the FHAct).

[24]   FED. FIN. INSTS. EXAMINATION COUNCIL, INTERAGENCY FAIR LENDING EXAMINATION PROCEDURES (Aug. 2009).

[25]   576 U.S. 519 (2015).

[26]   HUD, *Reinstatement of Discriminatory Effects Standard*, final rule (88 Fed. Reg. 19450, Mar. 31, 2023) [codified at 24 C.F.R. pt. 100].

[27]   Press Release, Dep't of Justice, Justice Department Announces New Initiative to Combat Redlining (Oct. 22, 2021).

[28]   Consent Order, *United States v. Lakeland Bank*, No. 2:22-cv-05746 (D.N.J. Sept. 29, 2022).

[29]   CFPB, CFPB, DOJ Order Trident Mortgage Company to Pay More Than $22 Million for Deliberate Discrimination Against Minority Families (July 27, 2022).

[30]   CFPB, Redlining: Consumer Financial Protection Bureau and Department Of Justice Action Requires Bancorpsouth To Pay $10.6 Million To Address Discriminatory Mortgage Lending Practices (June 29, 2016).

[31]   Stip. of Dismissal Pursuant to Settlement Agreement, *Schneiderman v. Evans Bancorp, Inc.*, No. 14-cv-00726 (W.D.N.Y. Sept. 11, 2015).

[32]   Press Release, N.Y. Att'y Gen. Eric T. Schneiderman, A.G. Schneiderman Secures Agreement With Evans Bank Ending Discriminatory Mortgage Redlining in Buffalo (Sept. 10, 2015); *see also* Jessica Silver-Greenberg, *New York Accuses Evans Bank of Redlining*, N.Y. TIMES, Sept. 2, 2014, http://dealbook.nytimes.com/2014/09/02/new-york-set-to-accuse-evans-bank-of-redlining/?_r=0.

[33]   New York State Dep't of Fin. Servs., Report on Inquiry into Redlining in Buffalo, New York (Feb. 4, 2021).

[34]   *See supra* note 20.

[35]   Consent Order, *United States v. Advocate Law Groups of Florida, P.A.*, No. 6:18-cv-1836 (M.D. Fla. June 10, 2022).

[36]   Order Granting Motion to Approve Consent Decree, *United States v. Auto Fare, Inc.*, No. 3:14-cv-00008 (W.D.N.C. Mar. 30, 2015).

[37]   *City of Oakland v. Wells Fargo & Co.*, 972 F.3d 1112, 1118 n.3 (9th Cir. 2020), *reh'g en banc granted, vacated*, 993 F.3d 1077 (9th Cir. 2021), *aff'd in part, rev'd in part & remanded* 14 F.4th 1030 (9th Cir. 2021).

[38]   Complaint, *Fair Hous. Justice Ctr., Inc. v. M&T Bank Corp.*, No. 15-cv-779 (S.D.N.Y. Feb. 3, 2014).

[39]   Fair Housing Justice Center, M&T Bank and FHJC Resolve Fair Housing Case (Sept. 1, 2015).

[40]   12 C.F.R. pt. 1002, 42 U.S.C. §§ 3601, *et seq.*

[41]   CFPB Synchrony Bank Consent Order, *supra* note 11.

[42]   Consent Order, *United States v. Trustmark Nat'l Bank*, No. 2:21-cv-2664 (W.D. Tenn. Oct. 27, 2021).

[43]   Complaint, *Bureau of Consumer Fin. Prot. v. Townstone Fin., Inc.*, No. 1:20-cv-04176 (N.D. Ill. July 10, 2020).

[44]   *See* Complaint, *United States & v. BancorpSouth Bank*, No. 1:16-cv-00118 (N.D. Miss. June 29, 2016).

[45]   *See* Consent Order, *United States v. BancorpSouth Bank*, No. 1:16-cv-00118 (N.D. Miss. July 25, 2016).

[46]   Consent Order, *Consumer Fin. Protection Bureau v. Nat'l City Bank*, No. 2:13-cv-01817 (W.D. Penn. Jan. 9, 2014).

[47]   *See, e.g.*, Press Release, Dep't of Justice, Justice Department Reaches Fair Lending Settlement with Chevy Chase Bank Resulting in $2.85 Million in Relief for Homeowners (Sept. 30, 2013); Press Release, Dep't of Justice, Justice Department Reaches Settlement with Southport Bank to Resolve Allegations of Mortgage Lending Discrimination (Sept. 26, 2013).

[48] Consent Order, *United States v. AIG Fed. Sav. Bank*, No. 1:10-cv-00178 (D. Del. Mar. 19, 2010).

[49] *Id.*

[50] Title VIII Conciliation Agreement, between U.S. Dep't of Hous. & Urban Dev. and Greenlight Fin. Servs., FHEO No. 09-13-0147-8 (June 5, 2014).

[51] *See* Dep't of Justice Press Release, *supra* note 7.

[52] CONSUMER FIN. PROT. BUREAU, CFPB BULL. NO. 2013-02, INDIRECT AUTO LENDING AND COMPLIANCE WITH THE EQUAL CREDIT OPPORTUNITY ACT (2013).

[53] *See* Chapter III for a discussion of the legal theories of discrimination.

[54] *See* Press Release, Consumer Fin. Prot. Bureau, Consumer Financial Protection Bureau Proposes New Federal Oversight of Nonbank Auto Finance Companies (Sept. 17, 2014); Defining Larger Participants of the Automobile Financing Market and Defining Certain Automobile Leasing Activity as a Financial Product or Service, 79 Fed. Reg. 60,762 (proposed Oct. 8, 2014); CONSUMER FIN. PROT. BUREAU, SUPERVISORY HIGHLIGHTS (2014); CONSUMER FIN. PROT. BUREAU, USING PUBLICLY AVAILABLE INFORMATION TO PROXY FOR UNIDENTIFIED RACE AND ETHNICITY: A METHODOLOGY AND ASSESSMENT (2014) [hereinafter CFPB White Paper].

[55] *See* CFPB Ally Consent Order, *supra* note 9.

[56] *See* Consent Order, *In re American Honda Finance Corporation*, File No. 2015-CFPB-0014 (July 14, 2015).

[57] *See* Consent Order, *In re Fifth Third Bank*, File No. 2015-CFPB-0024 (Sept. 28, 2015).

[58] *See* Consent Order, *In re Toyota Motor Credit Corporation*, File No. 2016-CFPB-0002 (Feb. 2, 2016).

[59] 5 U.S.C. § 801 *et seq.*

[60] Complaint, *Consumer Fin. Prot. Bureau v. Credit Acceptance Corp.*, No. 1:23cv38 (S.D.N.Y. Jan. 4, 2023).

[61] Consent Order Under New York Banking Law §§ 9-D and 39, *Chemung Canal Tr. Co.*, 2021 WL 5279603 (N.Y. Banking Dep't. June 21, 2021); Consent Order Under New York Banking Law §§ 9-D and 39, *Adirondack Tr. Co.*, 2021 WL 5279602 (N.Y. Banking Dep't. June 24, 2021); Consent Order, *Rhinebeck Bank* (N.Y. Banking Dep't. Oct. 5, 2022).

[62] *See, e.g.,* Richard Cordray, Director, Consumer Fin. Prot. Bureau, Prepared Remarks on the Payday/DAP Study Press Call (Apr. 24, 2013).

[63] The Pew Charitable Trusts, *Payday Lending in America: Who Borrows, Where They Borrow, and Why*, July 2012.

64   Consent Order, *In the Matter of ACE Cash Express, Inc.*, File No. 2014-CFPB-0008, July 8, 2014.

65   Consent Order, *In the Matter of EZ CORP, Inc., et al*, File No. 2015-CFPB-0031, Dec. 15, 2015.

66   Consent Order, *United States v. Nixon State Bank*, No. 5:11-cv-00488-FB (W.D. Tex. June 21, 2011).

67   Consent Order, *United States v. Fort Davis State Bank*, No. 4:13-cv-00077-RAJ (W.D. Tex. Dec. 19, 2013).

68   Consent Order, *United States v. First United Bank*, No. 3:15-cv-00144-L (N.D. Tex. Jan. 15, 2015).

69   David Skanderson & Dubravka Ritter, *Fair Lending Analysis of Credit Cards* (Fed. Reserve Bank of Phila., Payment Cards Ctr. Discussion Paper No. 14-02, 2014).

70   Simon Firestone, *Race, Ethnicity, and Credit Card Marketing*, 46 J. OF MONEY, CREDIT & BANKING 1205 (2014).

71   *See* Joint Consent Order, Joint Order for Restitution, and Joint Order to Pay Civil Money Penalty, *In re American Express Centurion Bank*, No. FDIC-12-315b, FDIC-12-316k, 2012-CFPB-0002 (Oct. 1, 2012); Joint Consent Order, *In re American Express Bank, FSB*, No. 2012-CFPB-0003 (Oct. 1, 2012); Joint Consent Order, *In re American Express Travel Related Services Company, Inc.*, No. 2012-CFPB-0004 (Oct. 1, 2012).

72   *See* Press Release, CFPB Orders American Express to Pay $85 Million Refund to Consumers Harmed by Illegal Credit Card Practices (Oct. 1, 2012) https://www.consumerfinance.gov/about-us/blog/cfpb-publishes-beginners-guide-to-accessing-and-using-home-mortgage-disclosure-act-data/.

73   In the FDIC's Consumer Compliance Supervisory Highlights report dated March 2022, the agency revealed that it had referred a fair lending matter to the DOJ involving a pattern or practice of discrimination in underwriting student loans. The FDIC determined that the institution's use of cohort default ratios in credit decisioning resulted in the "disproportionate exclusion" of students who attended Historically Black Colleges and Universities ("HBCUs") from applying for credit. Because graduates of HBCUs were disproportionately black, the FDIC concluded that the institution's policy of using the CDR had a disparate impact on the basis of race, and thus referred the matter to the DOJ.

74   CONSUMER FIN. PROT. BUREAU, EDUCATION LOAN EXAMINATION PROCEDURES 4 (2013).

75   *See, e.g., id.* at 10-12.

76   Joint Guidance on Overdraft Protection Programs, 70 Fed. Reg. 9,127, 9,131 (Feb. 24, 2005).

[77] FED. DEPOSIT INS. CORP., FDIC LETTER NO. FIL-81-2010, OVERDRAFT PAYMENT PROGRAMS AND CONSUMER PROTECTION: FINAL OVERDRAFT PAYMENT SUPERVISORY GUIDANCE (2010).

[78] CFPB, Request for Information Regarding Fees Imposed by Providers of Consumer Financial Products or Services (87 Fed. Reg. 5801, Feb. 2, 2022).

[79] CFPB, Consumer Financial Protection Circular 2022-06, *Unanticipated overdraft fee assessment practices*, Oct. 26, 2022.

[80] *See* Conciliation Agreement, *supra* note 17.

[81] *See* Press Release, *supra* note 18.

[82] *See* ANDREA MITCHELL & LORI SOMMERFIELD, AM. ASS'N OF BANK DIRS., RED FLAGS FOR FAIR LENDING RISK - HOW BANKS CAN IDENTIFY AND RESOLVE THEM (2012). Additional red flags include loan terms based on age differentiation, significant consumer complaints, negative examination or audit results, and changes in laws, rules, regulatory guidance, or regulatory expectations that make the products or services currently offered suspect.

[83] CFPB White Paper, *supra* note 54.

[84] *See* Agreed Order, *supra* note 13.

[85] *See* Jo Ann Barefoot & Lori J. Sommerfield, *Regulatory Relationship Management: Planning, Organizing and Managing Examinations*, 96 BNA's BANKING REP. 887 (May 10, 2011); Jo Ann Barefoot & Lori J. Sommerfield, *Regulatory Relationship Management: Building Trust, Credibility With Regulators*, 96 BNA BANKING REP. 18 (May 3, 2011).

[86] *See also* Andrew Sandler, Andrea Mitchell & Susanna Khalil, *A Practical Guide to CFPB Compliance Examination Management*, 29 REV. OF BANKING & FIN. SERVS. 125 (Oct. 2013).

[87] CFPB 2021 Fair Lending Report, at 2, available at: https://files.consumerfinance.gov/f/documents/cfpb_2021-fair-lending_report_2022-05.pdf.

[88] *Id.* at 4.

[89] Press Release, Consumer Fin. Prot. Bureau, The CFPB's 2021 Fair Lending Annual Report to Confress (May 6, 2022) (This press release accompanied the CFPB's 2021 Fair Lending Report, available at: https://www.consumerfinance.gov/about-us/blog/the-cfpbs-2021-fair-lending-annual-report-to-congress/).

[90] *Id.*

[91] 12 U.S.C. § 1828(x).

[92] In 2015, the CFPB adopted amendments to Regulation C that were designed to implement changes to HMDA required by the Dodd-Frank Act of 2010 and generally became effective on January 1, 2018. In the final rule, the Bureau modified the types of transactions subject to Regulation C. The

final rule adopted a dwelling-secured standard for all loans or lines of credit that are for personal, family, or household purposes. Thus, most consumer-purpose transactions (including closed-end home equity loans, home equity lines of credit, and reverse mortgages) are subject to the regulation. Notably, the final rule excludes from coverage home improvement loans that are not secured by a dwelling (i.e., home improvement loans that are unsecured or that are secured by some other type of collateral).

[93]   For additional information regarding reportable HMDA data, *see* CFPB, *Reportable HMDA Data: A Regulatory and Reporting Overview Reference Chart for HMDA Data Collected in 2022* (effective Jan. 1, 2022), https://files.consumerfinance.gov/f/documents/cfpb_2022-reportable-hmda-data.pdf.

[94]   For additional information regarding LAR format, *see* FED. FIN. INSTS. EXAMINATION COUNCIL, A GUIDE TO HMDA REPORTING: GETTING IT RIGHT! (2022), https://www.ffiec.gov/hmda/pdf/2022Guide.pdf.

[95]   The CFPB's FFIEC HMDA Filing Platform is available at https://ffiec.cfpb.gov/.

[96]   The FFIEC is an interagency body that establishes uniform principles, standards, and report forms for the federal examination of financial institutions by the Board of Governors of the Federal Reserve System, the Federal Deposit Insurance Corporation (FDIC), the National Credit Union Administration (NCUA), the Office of the Comptroller of the Currency (OCC), and the Consumer Financial Protection Bureau (CFPB). In 2006, the State Liaison Committee (SLC) became a voting member of the FFIEC. *See* https://www.ffiec.gov/.

[97]   The tool is available on the CFPB's website at http://www.consumerfinance.gov/hmda/.

[98]   Press Release, CFPB Publishes Beginner's Guide to Accessing and Using Home Mortgage Disclosure Act Data (June 13, 2022).

[99]   For purposes of Regulation C, any lender that meets the definition of a "financial institution" (as defined in 12 C.F.R. § 1003.2) is required to collect HMDA data and file a LAR by March 1 of each calendar year. *See* 12 C.F.R. §§ 1003.4, 1003.5(a).

[100]   CONSUMER FIN. PROT. BUREAU, CFPB BULL. NO. 2013-11, HOME MORTGAGE DISCLOSURE ACT (HMDA) AND REGULATION C – COMPLIANCE MANAGEMENT; CFPB HMDA RESUBMISSION SCHEDULE AND GUIDELINES; HMDA ENFORCEMENT (2013), and HMDA EXAMINATION PROCEDURES, COMPLIANCE MANAGEMENT REVIEW (Aug. 2017).

[101]   FFIEC, HMDA EXAMINER TRANSACTION TESTING GUIDELINES (2017), https://files.consumerfinance.gov/f/documents/201708_cfpb_ffiec-hmda-examiner-transaction-testing-guidelines.pdf; see also CFPB, Here's what you need to know about the new FFIEC HMDA Examiner Transaction Testing Guidelines (Aug. 22, 2017), https://www.consumerfinance.gov/about-us/blog/heres-what-you-need-

know-about-new-ffiec-hmda-examiner-transaction-testing-guidelines/. In 2022, the CFPB issued a blog post noting that a federal district court decision modified the threshold for reporting data on closed-end mortgage loans. The threshold for reporting such data is now 25 loans in each of the two preceding calendar years, which is the threshold established by the 2015 HMDA Final Rule, rather than the 100 loan threshold set by the 2020 HMDA Final Rule. CFPB, Changes to HMDA's closed-end loan reporting threshold (Dec. 6, 2022).

102   Nationstar Mortgage, LLC d/b/a Mr. Cooper, CFPB No. 2017-CFPB-0011 (Mar. 15, 2017).

103   Freedom Mortgage Corporation, CFPB No. 2019-BCFP-0007 (June 5, 2019).

104   Washington Federal Bank, N.A., CFPB No. 2013-CFPB-0005 (Oct. 9, 2013); Washington Federal Bank, N.A., CFPB No. 2020-BCFP-0019 (Oct. 27, 2020).

105   See, e.g., Nationstar Mortgage, LLC d/b/a Mr. Cooper, CFPB No. 2017-CFPB-0011 (Mar. 15, 2017); Washington Federal Bank, N.A., CFPB No. 2013-CFPB-0005 (Oct. 9, 2013); Washington Federal Bank, N.A., CFPB No. 2020-BCFP-0019 (Oct. 27, 2020).

106   12 C.F.R. § 1003.6(b)(1).

107   See e.g., Cty. of Cook v. HSBC N. Am. Holdings, Inc., 314 F. Supp. 3d 950, 956 (N.D. Ill. 2018) (Plaintiff utilized HMDA data as evidence of HSBC's pricing disparities for minority borrowers in support of Plaintiff's allegation that HSBC discriminatorily targeted minority homeowners with subprime mortgage loans).

108   633 F. Supp. 2d 922 (N.D. Cal. 2008).

109   Ramirez v. GreenPoint Mortg. Funding, Inc., 268 F.R.D. 627 (N.D. Cal. 2010).

110   See e.g., Emmanuel Martinez and Aaron Glantz, Kept Out: How we identified lending disparities in federal mortgage data, REVEAL (Feb. 15, 2018), https://revealnews.org/article/how-we-identified-lending-disparities-in-federal-mortgage-data/.

111   Conciliation Agreement, between Metro. St. Louis Equal Hous. Opportunity Council and First Nat'l Bank of St. Louis, FHEO No. 07-10-0152-8 (Dec. 21, 2010).

112   CFPB 2014 Fair Lending Report, at 4, 14, available at: https://files.consumerfinance.gov/f/201504_cfpb_fair_lending_report.pdf.

113   12 C.F.R. §§ 1002.5, 1002.13.

114   12 C.F.R. § 1003.4.

115   12 C.F.R. § 1003.1(b)(iii).

[116]   12 C.F.R. § 1002.5(b); *see* Settlement Agreement & Order, *United States v. Fidelity Fed. Bank*, FSB, No. 1:02-cv-03906 (E.D.N.Y. July 25, 2002).

[117]   CFPB Ally Consent Order, *supra* note 9; Consent Order, *United States v. Ally Fin. Inc.*, No. 2:13-cv-15180 (E.D. Mich. Dec. 23, 2013); American Honda Finance Corporation, CFPB No. 2015-CFPB-0014 (July 14, 2015); Consent Order, *United States v. Am. Honda Fin. Corp.*, No. 2:15-cv-05264 (C.D. Cal. July 16, 2015); Fifth Third Bank, CFPB No. 2015-CFPB-0024 (Sept. 28, 2015); Consent Order, *United States v. Fifth Third Bank*, No. 1:15-cv-626 (S.D. Ohio Sept. 28, 2015).

[118]   Marc N. Elliott et al., *Using the Census Bureau's Surname List to Improve Estimates of Race/Ethnicity and Associated Disparities*, 9 HEALTH SERVS. & OUTCOMES RESEARCH METHODOLOGY 69 (Apr. 10, 2009).

[119]   CFPB White Paper, *supra* note 54.

[120]   Elliott et al., *supra* note 118.

[121]   ARTHUR P. BAINES & DR. MARSHA J. COURCHANE, AM. FIN. SERVS. ASS'N, FAIR LENDING: IMPLICATIONS FOR THE INDIRECT AUTO FINANCE MARKET (2014).

[122]   *Id.* at 56.

[123]   *Id.*

[124]   FED. FIN. INSTS. EXAMINATION COUNCIL, *supra* note 24, at app. 19.

[125]   CONSUMER FIN. PROT. BUREAU, CFPB BULL. NO. 2013-06, RESPONSIBLE BUSINESS CONDUCT: SELF-POLICING, SELF-REPORTING, REMEDIATION AND COOPERATION (2013).

[126]   12 C.F.R. § 1080.6(c).

[127]   12 C.F.R. § 1080.6(e).

[128]   12 C.F.R. § 1080.6(g).

[129]   With the CFPB, for example, this is called a PARR letter in the event of a preliminary supervisory determination or a Notice and Opportunity to Respond and Advise ("NORA") letter in the event of an investigation arising out of the enforcement division. As noted above, the prudential regulators typically issue a 15-day letter.

[130]   Equal Credit Opportunity Act, Pub. L. No. 93-495, § 502, 88 Stat. 1521 (1974) (emphasis added).

[131]   Equal Credit Opportunity Act Amendments of 1976, Pub. L. No. 94-239, § 2, 90 Stat. 251 (1976).

[132]   15 U.S.C. § 1691(a)(1)-(3). A creditor means "a person who, in the ordinary course of business, regularly participates in a credit decision, including setting the terms of the credit...." 12 C.F.R. § 1002.2(l).

[133]   12 C.F.R. pt. 1002, supp. I (CFPB, Official Staff Interpretations).

[134]   15 U.S.C. § 1691c(a).

[135]   15 U.S.C. § 1691c(c).

[136]   15 U.S.C. § 1691e.

[137]   15 U.S.C. § 1691e(g).

[138]   12 U.S.C. § 5514(c)(3)

[139]   Despite the narrower circumstances in which violations are required to be referred to DOJ under ECOA (*see* 15 U.S.C. § 1691e(g)), the prudential regulators and the CFPB generally refer all potential pattern or practice discrimination matters to the DOJ.

[140]   133 S. Ct. 2675 (2013).

[141]   Memorandum from CFPB Director Richard Cordray to CFPB Staff (June 25, 2014) [hereinafter CFPB Memorandum], http://files.consumerfinance.gov/f/201407_cfpb_memo_ensuring-equal-treatment-for-same-sex-married-couples.pdf.   It is noteworthy that the CFPB's guidance took the unusual form of a memorandum to CFPB staff, rather than a bulletin or an interpretive rule subject to the Administrative Procedure Act's public and notice requirements.   In February 2014, DOJ also issued a similar memorandum to its employees.   Memorandum from the Attorney General to All Department of Justice Employees, Department Policy on Ensuring Equal Treatment for Same-Sex Married Couples (Feb. 10, 2014).

[142]   *Windsor*, 133 S. Ct. at 2683 (quoting 1 U.S.C. § 7).

[143]   CFPB Memorandum, *supra* note 141, at 1.

[144]   140 S. Ct. 1731 (2020).

[145]   CFPB, Interpretive Rule, Equal Credit Opportunity (Regulation B); Discrimination on the Bases of Sexual Orientation and Gender Identity (86 Fed. Reg. 14363, Mar. 16, 2021).

[146]   Although the FHAct uses the terminology "handicap," HUD now uses the modern term "disability" on its website to describe this prohibited basis.

[147]   *See generally* 42 U.S.C. §§ 3608-3612 (HUD administration and enforcement of the FHAct); 42 U.S.C. § 3614 (DOJ enforcement of the FHAct).

[148]   Exec. Order No. 12,892, 59 Fed. Reg. 2,939 (Jan. 17, 1994).

[149]   42 U.S.C. § 3614(a).

[150]   42 U.S.C. § 3610(a)(1)(A).

[151]   42 U.S.C. § 3610(a)(1)(A); 42 U.S.C. § 3612(o).

[152]   Equal Access to Housing in HUD Programs Regardless of Sexual Orientation or Gender Identity, 77 Fed. Reg. 5,662 (Feb. 3, 2012); 24 C.F.R. § 5.105(a)(2).

[153] Executive Order 13988 on Preventing and Combating Discrimination on the Basis of Gender Identity or Sexual Orientation.

[154] U.S. Dept. of Housing & Urban Dev., Memorandum re: Implementation of Executive Order 13988 on the Enforcement of the Fair Housing Act (Feb. 11, 2021).

[155] 21 Palms RV Resort, Inc. and Nathan Dykgraaf, HUDOHA No. 22-AF-0181-FH-010 (Aug. 31, 2022).

[156] 24 C.F.R. § 100.500(c)(2).

[157] 135 S. Ct. 2507 (2011).

[158] It is important to note that the U.S. Supreme Court's opinion in *Inclusive Communities* did not specifically dictate the standards and burdens of proof that apply to the burden-shifting test in disparate impact claims. However, the Court's opinion emphasized proper limitations on the use of disparate impact to avoid serious constitutional questions and to protect defendants against "abusive" disparate impact claims. *Tex. Dep't of Hous. & Cmty. Affairs v. Inclusive Cmtys. Project, Inc.*, 135 S. Ct. 2507, 2511 (2011).

With regard to the first step of the burden-shifting framework, the Court reaffirmed the significant burden on the plaintiff in establishing a *prima facie* case. The Court stated that a "robust causality requirement" is important, and that plaintiffs relying on a statistical disparity must show that a specific policy of defendant caused the disparity. *Id.* In the second step, in which the burden shifts to the defendant to refute the allegation, the Court determined that defendants in disparate impact cases must be given an opportunity to state and explain the valid interests served by their policies, and that those policies should be allowed if the defendants can demonstrate they are necessary to achieve a legitimate objective. Citing the seminal case of *Griggs v. Duke Power*, the Court stated that policies are not contrary to the disparate impact requirement unless they are "artificial, arbitrary, and unnecessary barriers." 401 U.S. 424, 431 (1971). In the third step, the Court indicated that before a business justification can be rejected, the plaintiff must show that there is "an available alternative . . . practice that has less disparate impact and services the [entity's] legitimate needs." *Inclusive Cmtys.*, 135 S. Ct. at 2511 (quoting *Ricci v. DeStefano*, 557 U.S. 557, 578 (2009)). Finally, the Court noted that when courts do find liability under a disparate impact theory, their remedial orders should concentrate on the elimination of the practice.

[159] 85 Fed. Reg. 60288.

[160] 87 Fed. Reg 33884 (June 3, 2022).

[161] 12 U.S.C. §§ 2801–2810; 12 C.F.R. §§ 1003.1-1003.6.

[162] FED. FIN. INSTS. EXAMINATION COUNCIL, *supra* note 94.

[163] *See supra* Chapter VIII.

[164] The CFPB has expanded its interpretation of responsible lending laws by ensuring that banking financial products and services provide value to consumers commensurate with the costs. For example, one of the CFPB's recurring enforcement action themes has been ensuring that credit card "add-on products," such as debt protection, identity theft protection, and credit scoring tracking, represent fair value to consumers.

In conjunction with the CFPB's first credit card add-on product enforcement action in 2012, the Bureau released Bulletin 2012-06 (Marketing of Credit Card Add-On Products), which signaled to the industry that the CFPB was looking very closely at UDAAP issues in marketing and sales practices in the credit card markets. CONSUMER FIN. PROT. BUREAU, CFPB BULL. NO. 2012-06, MARKETING OF CREDIT CARD ADD-ON PRODUCTS (July 18, 2012). Implied within that guidance is the concept that consumers should receive real value for the add-on products they agree to purchase. Therefore, banks that market and sell credit card add-on products should closely review that guidance and evaluate their own practices to take corrective action as needed. Particular consideration should be given to processes for assessing whether a product or service and its terms and conditions provide fair, tangible value to consumers and satisfy regulatory concerns about the potential for consumer harm.

[165] 12 U.S.C. § 45.

[166] 12 U.S.C. §§ 5531, 5536. We also note that the Servicemembers Civil Relief Act ("SCRA") is at times considered a "responsible lending" law. 50 U.S.C. §§ 3901 – 4043. The SCRA, which was amended by Congress in 2003, is designed to ease certain financial burdens for servicemembers on active duty military service. The SCRA is not addressed in this Handbook. By statute, only the DOJ has express authority to enforce the SCRA. *See* 50 U.S.C. § 4041. The prudential regulators, CFPB, FTC, and Department of Defense ("DOD"), however, are also actively concerned with servicemember protections involving financial products and services. The prudential regulators, CFPB, and FTC may refer cases to the DOJ for enforcement, work in coordination with the DOJ on enforcement actions, or even take affirmative action on their own to enforce SCRA despite the lack of express statutory authority

[167] For example, CFPB Director Richard Cordray explained during Congressional testimony in 2012 that the determination of what practices are abusive "is going to have to be a fact and circumstances issue," and that it would "not be useful to try to define a term like that in the abstract." *How Will the CFPB Function Under Richard Cordray: Hearing before the Subcomm. on TARP, Fin. Servs., and Bailouts of Pub. & Private Programs*, 112th Cong. 112-107 (2012) (statement of Richard Cordray, Director, Consumer Fin. Prot. Bureau).

Since 2012, the CFPB has undertaken several enforcement actions involving abusive practices. In one case, for example, the CFPB alleged that Ace Cash Express, Inc. ("Ace") used illegal debt collection tactics with respect to its payday lending services. Specifically, the Bureau alleged that

Ace engaged in abusive conduct by creating an "artificial sense of urgency" to pressure delinquent consumers to pay off their existing payday loans and then immediately take out a new payday loan with accompanying fees, even though borrowers had already demonstrated an inability to repay. The CFPB believed these tactics took unreasonable advantage of the inability of consumers to protect their own interests in selecting or using a consumer financial product or service. Ace agreed to pay $5 million in consumer restitution and a $5 million civil money penalty. Ace Cash Express, Inc., CFPB No. 2014-CFPB-0008 (July 8, 2014).

[168]   CFPB, Statement of Policy Regarding Prohibition on Abusive Acts or Practices (Jan. 24, 2020)
https://files.consumerfinance.gov/f/documents/cfpb_abusiveness-enforcement-policy_statement.pdf.

[169]   *Id.*

[170]   CFPB, Statement of Policy Regarding Prohibition on Abusive Acts or Practices; Rescission (Mar. 11, 2021).

[171]   CFPB, Policy Statement on Abusive Practices, 88 Fed. Reg. 21883 (Apr. 12, 2023).

[172]   CFPB, CFPB Targets Unfair Discrimination in Consumer Finance (March 16, 2022) https://www.consumerfinance.gov/about-us/newsroom/cfpb-targets-unfair-discrimination-in-consumer-finance/.

[173]   CFPB, Unfair, Deceptive, or Abusive Acts or Practices Exam Manual (March 2022) https://files.consumerfinance.gov/f/documents/cfpb_unfair-deceptive-abusive-acts-practices-udaaps_procedures.pdf.

[174]   *Id.*

[175]   CFPB, *supra* note 172.

Made in United States
Troutdale, OR
10/10/2023

13578998R00090